MINI
COOPER *and* S

MINI

COOPER *and* S

997 & 998 Cooper; 970, 1071 & 1275S

Jeremy Walton

MOTORBOOKS
INTERNATIONAL

This edition published in 2004 by Motorbooks International, an imprint of MBI Publishing Company, Galtier Plaza, Suite 200, 380 Jackson Street, St. Paul, MN 55101-3885 U.S.A.

First published in 1982 by Osprey Publishing Limited.

The information in this book is true and complete to the best of our knowledge. All recommendations are made without any guarantee on the part of the author or Publisher, who also disclaim any liability incurred in connection with the use of this data or specific details.

We recognize that some words, model names and designations, for example, mentioned herein are the property of the trademark holder. We use them for identification purposes only. This is not an
official publication.

Motorbooks International titles are also available at discounts in bulk quantity for industrial or sales-promotional use. For details write to Special Sales Manager at Motorbooks International Wholesalers & Distributors, Galtier Plaza, Suite 200, 380 Jackson Street, St. Paul, MN 55101-3885 U.S.A.

ISBN 0-7603-1982-0

Printed in Hong Kong

Contents

Chapter 1
A mini in search of power

August 1959: Cliff Richard dominated the British Summer with a ditty entitled *Living Doll*. Harold Macmillan was in full flight working on a legend for the nation that they had 'never had it so good,' during a tenure as Prime Minister that was to last into the sixties. Now, 21 years to the month, later I write this in a Britain entrusted to the premiership of the lady, Margaret Thatcher and EMI are still doing very nicely, thank you, from the works of Mr C. Richard. Linking 21 equally tumultuous years of the British motor industry is the Mini.

Then it was a fresh-faced little baby box. An unsophisticated exterior, wearing seams and door hinges for all to see. Yet underneath was a transverse engined, front-driven phenomenon that has literally changed the face of the world's motor industry, or at least the mechanical underpinnings on which that industry depends.

The sheer space saving potential of turning the engine sideways and driving the front wheels took a while to sink in. At that time the big names in the European car business, including the British Motor Corporation, the Mini's original parent, relied either on front engine and rear drive or—especially on the Continent—one followed the Fiat, Volkswagen and Renault school of rear engine, rear drive.

Then the most basic 848 cc/34 bhp Mini cost £497, to the nearest pound. There was a basic choice between two offerings: Austin Seven, made at Longbridge, where Mini production continues in 1981. Or the Cowley manufactured Morris Mini Minor. Both had everything but the badge, the grille and colour choice in common. All round independent suspension via those ingenious rubber cones, to four wheel drum brakes within those tiny 10 in. diameter wheels. More commonly they were sold in slightly better trimmed de luxe form for a princely £537.

Today, in the wake of the tremendously successful Mini Metro launch, the choice of Minis is down to three models again all powered by a 39 bhp version of the 988 engine, an engine which shares some basics with a Cooper power unit of the sixties that we shall soon be discussing.

In those 21 years, the Mini has certainly become a legend in its own time. Some 4.8 million were sold in that period, but production dropped

Many Mini-Coopers went back to this bare body form before reassembly as competition cars. The Mini's inherent light weight and tiny external dimensions were very handy attributes for sports use. The strength of the body has been repeatedly proved in all sorts of spectacular accidents too!

The base from which Mini-Coopers were derived, clearly displaying the transverse engine, side radiator and later Hydrolastic suspension

in the wake of Metro. As I write the car was taking 2 to $2\frac{1}{2}$ per cent of the UK market, instead of its previous 5 to 6 per cent and capacity of the sole major manufacturing source (Longbridge) looked unlikely to reach 1000 units *a week*. Put in perspective, Ford have an Anglo-German capacity of double that, *per day*, for the new Escort and are seeking more.

In those 21 years every conceivable type of Mini has been made. The most famous derivatives, and the most emotive, were undoubtedly the Cooper and Cooper S types that form the basis of this book. Who can forget the inexpensive vans and pick-ups? They were still in production at close to £3000 when this was written. Remember the tax free £360 originals? Then the cheapest way of getting four new wheels capable of 70 (strictly illegal in Britain) mph, coupled to cornering capability that shamed most contemporary sports cars.

Or the Mini Moke? A vehicle which is loved in some remote spots of the world, and still the inspiration for all kinds of crazy fibreglass imitations of uncertain parentage.

A year and a month after the original was spawned the Estate was announced complete with genuine wood finish (or, as Dame Edna Everage would have it, 'look a cute little half-timbered car!'). In the autumn of 1961 we were offered another typically British option: a Riley or Wolseley badged model.

This time the badges also denoted modified styling (stubby little tailfins plus stick-on boot on a ten foot car, yet!), extra trim that included radiator grille, and extra weight. Up to 100 pounds of it, that demanded a bigger engine. But then, the Mini always demanded a bigger engine! From the start its miraculous way of scuttling round corners put a cheeky grin on some unlikely faces. From royalty down to the merely trendy, the Mini became *the* chic car, but something more than that was needed to make it a real sales success, even in Britain.

Looking back, motorsport and the Mini seemed made for each other. The international cocktail that made up the lineage of Sir Alec Issigonis— born in Turkey of Greek-descent, with a father of British nationality and Bavarian mother, is just part of his cosmopolitan background—also provided a strong competitive streak. This free-thinking engineer had the gift of sketching out his

A beautifully presented and polished example of the Mini-Cooper S A-series four cylinder, twin SU carburettors gleaming. Keeping a motor in this condition once installed is a different matter, that 16 blade fan capable of swirling the road dirt that passes in so easily from the grille, all over such conscientious handwork

Final drive arrangements and those of the gearbox followed the Mini principles, but different ratios were specified for production Coopers and there were very efficient straight-cut gear sets for competition—so long as the occupants could stand the noise

ideas with the fluidity that has been likened to that of Leonardo da Vinci.

Issigonis constructed his own competition machinery (including the Lightweight Special with George Dowson) in the years subsequent to owning his first serious sporting machine, a

Alec Issigonis at the original 1959 Mini presentation, which was held on a military test track in Surrey

11

supercharged Ulster Austin. Thus he always understood, from a practical as well as theoretical viewpoint, the importance of low vehicle weight, structural stiffness and outstanding cornering capability. In competition straightline engine potential is often less important than cornering power. Today's Formula 1 GP racers are often slower on the straights than the narrow-wheeled 600 horsepower monsters that came from Germany in the thirties. Yet there is absolutely no comparison in circuit lap times, as the effect of huge, sticky, tyres and ground effect aerodynamics have slashed times beyond belief, even on circuits where there is a chance to run the maximum speed for more than split seconds. The Mini, and more particularly the Mini-Cooper illustrated the same point vividly, both in saloon car racing and rallying. Rallying's premium on predictable handling in unexpected circumstances allowed a major winning record to be maintained a little longer than in racing, where the introduction of ever wider wheels (filtering down from the Formula cars) enabled conventional rivals like Ford to endow the Anglia, and then the Cortina and Escort with extra instant cornering power. Then the limitations of front drive for transmitting power through tiny wheels started to matter. The end of the model's competition career was in sight, merely postponed by factory racing modifications like 12 in. diameter wheels and fuel injected versions of 1293cc that spat out over 135 bhp by 1970.

A far cry from a fuel-efficient 30 bhp or so initial answer to the post Suez petrol price/supply consciousness that the original Mini provided!

In the months following that August 1959 Mini announcement, BMC management worried over their bold little car's fortunes. They had been afraid that people would laugh at their box-like baby: in some places they did, though more at the low price BMC were charging for such advanced small car technology, rather than at an obviously logical answer to low cost transporation.

BMC had a sales problem on their hands in that the Mini cost only a little bit less than a conventional small car like the Austin A40 and its advantages, notably the delightful handling, were not immediately apparent on paper. The promise of 50 mpg was real enough for careful drivers, and it took determination to drag the little box down below 40 mpg. Powerful sales points, even more valid today!

General consensus of opinion in books written about the car was that it was its adoption by those fashionable elements in society which made the difference. That, and competition, for the first Minis were blooded quickly. This highlighted some fundamental problems, like the need for stronger steel wheels, which cracked under the strain of then-unbelievable cornering speeds. Three-wheeling antics, and the like, were needed to offset the aerodynamic (what aerodynamics? 'Like a barn door!' in the words of a legendary wisecrack by Henry Manney III) and gear train power losses. These meant that even a tuned 850 Mini was slower along the straights than class rivals from DKW, Fiat and Renault.

Reading back through that classic practical preparation guide, *Tuning a Mini* by the late Clive Trickey, I was amazed that the Mini ever got anywhere at all. Clive's writing style was always pungent—and always kept our telephones at *Cars and Car Conversions*' editorial department busy with outraged manufacturers and goody suppliers—but it was based on first hand experience. He also drove faster than many of his detractors, despite the asthma that led to his early death.

This very interesting shot was taken at the 1964 Olympia Racing Car Show. It reveals the architects of the Mini-Cooper, from left to right they are: Bill Appleby (BMC's chief engine designer) who is split from the background Daniel Richmond by the little old lady. Our next rail-gripper is the man who gave the car its name, John Cooper, with Charles Griffin (chassis design chief) and Sir Alec next to the Monte winner

These are excerpts from his comments on the original cars, for competition or hard road use . . . 'Rather crude 848 cc form. Often criticised because it just could not keep the water out and possessed one of the worst gearboxes and most inefficient set of brakes ever contrived. The roadholding was then, as it is now, phenomenal. Often rapid and complete failure of the standard shock absorbers. The first Mini engine tuners found the crankshaft very shortlived, timing gear and clutches even shorter lived. It was found that, since the camshaft ran directly in the block

without white metal bearings, it would seize and cause a wrecked engine unless these bearings were fitted.' And so on, but it didn't deter ordinary 850 owners like myself from visiting the choice of 50 or so tuners, varying in competence from the Issigonis confidants, respected for their ability like Daniel Richmond and racing car constructor John Cooper, down to the nearest back yard bodger with a lathe and power drill. Certainly the crank on my own 1965 850 broke. But the $1\frac{1}{2}$ in. single SU modified Mini was 'wedged up' the boot of a Rover 2000 travelling along the then com-

Just one of the more obscure Mini-derivatives that were sold around the world, this Moke-like model actually came from Australia despite the Americana decalling

15

paratively new M4 when it did break! And the
speedometer was wavering through the fuel
gauge that existed beyond the 90 mph section of
the large, central speedo, bidding for a complete
circuit back to zero again at the time.

Away from such teenage behaviour, how did
the works see it? Talking to some of the legendary
Abingdon wizards before the move to Cowley in
the summer of 1981, I heard that they didn't really
take the 850 seriously. This showed in the fact
that the hot shots in the works team were kept
clear of the 850s, but one of the earliest recorded
wins for the Mini—Knowldale CC's Mini
Miglia—went to Pat Moss (now married to Erik
Carlsson, but still an English resident) and Stuart
Turner. That was before Mr. Turner co-drove
Carlsson's front drive, two-stroke, Saab to RAC
victory. He then turned his hand to managing the
BMC works team in the Mini's heyday departing
via a spell at Castrol to Ford, where he entered the
'eighties as Director of Public Affairs. He was a
key Mini-Cooper figure because it was his natural
talent for aggressive planning and picking the
right team that kept the Mini on top in international rallies, years after Ford and others
should have been trampling on the Mini's competition grave.

Amongst those who did the unglamorous, but
vital, job of finding out about the Mini in big time
rallying—and what needed fixing to make it an
effective rally car—were Pat 'Tish' Ozanne, Alick
Pitts and Ken James. All were loaned works cars
for the 1959 RAC (not then a full blooded forest
event), but none finished, the dreaded slipping
clutch ailment having struck.

The Mini did survive both a Portuguese and a
first Monte Carlo foray (in 1960, one was a
dishevelled 73rd overall)! Yet the works per-
sisted, not as a front line winner, but just as

factory teams do get interested in exploring the merits of any new cars, for there will nearly always be more financial support to help sales.

Their reward came in the 1960 Geneva Rally when Don and Erle Morley scored a class win over Carlsson's Saab and two works DKWs, both also had front drive, two stroke, three-cylinder power.

BMC were getting somewhere, but not very fast! Through 1960 the majority of results tended toward the mediocre, with the inevitable teething troubles of any new car, especially one that combined such technical innovations. And yet, there was Tommy Gold's remarkable 14th overall, class-winning performance on the Alpine. An event where the Mini's remarkable handling must

History does not record whether the Canadians were grateful for the supply of side-striped, high-bumper Minis for the State of Ontario—whose 1973 motto was 'Keep it beautiful!'

17

Pioneering rally Minis looked like this, complete with three auxiliary lamps and top straps to the headlamps. This example is out on the 1961 RAC Rally

Right *the classic Mini rally picture, which was somewhat ironically taken during a televised special stage event that substituted for the cancelled 1967 RAC Rally: Timo Makinen is the driver, and this Mini had fuel injection*

have been stretched to the limit to offset the uphill hairpin climbing sections. And then, there was a marvellous sixth overall on the 1960 RAC Rally for David Seigle-Morris. Sure, Carlsson won the event in a similarly diminutive-engined car, but much bigger-bodied, fwd machine—but BMC could now see the potential in this tiny terror.

Rallying was changing in Britain too. The era of forest events, Scandinavian drivers and techniques and of viciously professional team managership was dawning.

A similarly efficient Mini was needed.

Chapter 2
997 Cooper – the legend begins

It took 23 months of enthusiastic Mini production before the first factory sports versions were ready. A whole new generation of cars, small, light and with more powerful engines driving agile front drive chassis, were then born in the years after that July 1961 announcement of the 997 cc Mini-Cooper. In its wake came other Coopers, the neglected 998 model that replaced the 997 and the attention-grabbing, original homologation specials: the Cooper S types. That they turned into genuine mass-production derivatives showed their inherent, and entertaining, worth.

You can see the aftermath still in the 'eighties. Volkswagen's Golf GTI is an extension of the theme, though with a bias toward charming road performance that was part of 997 Cooper philosophy, but not of the original competition-required Cooper S-types. The practice of linking famous names, as with double World Champion F1 constructor (1959–60) John Cooper's and the Mini was then very common. Yet, when the question of offering a high performance Mini-Metro as a Cooper came up in 1981, BL turned it down in favour of resuscitating the MG marque. A company spokesman told me, 'I and others like me, fought tooth and nail to get a Metro-Cooper off the ground inside the company, but it was felt MG was the more effective name now: Cooper just hasn't got the widespread pulling power it had in the sixties.' The Metro-Cooper project continued with John Cooper gaining backing from large Leyland outlet Wadham Stringer at first.

Cooper himself must have reflected how fast the performance world changes. As he drove back from the July 1981 British GP at the wheel of one of his defiantly stripy Metros, it was an ironic twenty years since his enthusiasm had carried both Issigonis—who was reluctant at first, having designed the Mini as a cheap people's car—and senior BMC management, into producing a high performance Mini.

What did you get?

The 997 Mini-Cooper introduced a number of desirable extras to Mini motoring, but not all of them worked as well as our rose-tinted retrospective spectacles might have us believe. Features, aside from a 1-litre/55 bhp motor, included front disc brakes, remote gearchange and closer ratio gears for first, second and third.

Most important in a car that was not going to change shape in a performance version—unlike today's heavily spoilered performance descendants such as the Ford Escort XR3—was extra power. That could have come from simply tweaking up the 850, but it wasn't noted for ruggedness under duress, and there was an obvious, though expensive, alternative.

John Cooper was not only at the forefront of GP racing, he had a link with BMC through his activities in 1-litre Formula Junior single-seater racing. The best powerplant for this category had evolved as a BMC A-series, the four cylinder pushrod valve gear principles of which all-iron engines live on in the Metro of the eighties.

Cooper knew a lot about this engine in 1-litre,

Original 1961 Morris Mini-Cooper 997 represents Britain almost as characteristically as the thatched house in the background. Note the contrasting roof colour (black with red in this case) and the retention of C41 cross ply tyres on early production cars. Instant frontal recognition was assured by the prominent grille bars and modest badging changes. Trim levels were as for the better equipped ordinary Minis, including opening rear windows

80 bhp racing trim. It was decided that to get the required 85 mph straightline speed in a Mini, some proven racing technology could be used to produce a comparatively lowly 55 bhp with more durability and flexibility than were offered by 848 cc.

Capacity grew expensively, with a long stroke crankshaft contributing to the Mini-Cooper's slightly smaller bore (62.43 mm compared to 850's 62.94 mm) and tooth-trembling long stroke (81.28 mm versus 850's 68.26 mm). Not surprisingly the crankshaft was strengthened, including an eighth of an inch on the flywheel-supporting output section of the shaft, and increased crankshaft web thickness. The original 997s had an oilway drilled into the crank, beneath the primary gear, but the most important durability asset was felt to be the crankshaft vibration damper, which also alleviated some earlier enthusiasts' grumbles about the timing gear's reliability at rpm beyond 6000. Lead indium bearings were specified; very necessary as peak power had been moved 500 rpm up

Larger bore single exhaust pipe and minor badge change to Morris Cooper were the easiest rear recognition symbols of the long stroke 997 cc Coopers, but the contrasting roof panel colour also established a tradition (but by no means mandatory) for Cooper and Cooper S

the scale exhibited by the 850 and peak torque value was up from 2900 to 3600 revs.

Domed pistons increased compression from the normal 850 ratio of 8.3:1 to 9:1. That higher compression ratio was complemented by a thorough revision of the engine's breathing abilities.

Externally the pair of HS2 SU 1.25 in. carburettors were *the* Mini under-bonnet status symbols of the time. They were mounted at a slightly inclined angle and, as usual on the A-series, were on the same side as the exhaust system, which had also been replaced by a three branch tubular manifold or larger bore. Naturally this increase in pipe size was continued to the single large bore tailpipe,

Complete with whitewall tyres the Austin Cooper goes on display at the 1961 Paris Show. The board refers to an endurance run that the 'Baby-Austin' had completed on the 28 September 1961, managing 1627 Km at average speeds of 80 mph plus with four passengers on board

25

The 1961 underbonnet layout displays the original sports air filters for the twin 1¼ in SU carburettors. This is the Morris version defined by the larger grille slats than its Austin counterpart

one of the few external features—aside from badging and the wide, horizontal, bars of the front grille—that give the Cooper game away.

Internally the new long stroke motor gained a camshaft then coded 948. It included a valve lift of 0.312 in. to replace the usual 850's 0.280 in. and a 252 degree camshaft duration compared with the previous 230 degree. Valve sizes, inlet only, were increased modestly, and double springs used to extend the rpm range to 6000—and beyond, if you weren't paying the bills! Incidentally the head

and valve gear, plus the SUs, were originally designed for the Mk II Sprite.

The effect of these changes was to provide that 55 bhp, some 16 extra horsepower than previously available from the production lines. Again there were Austin and Morris versions, but only one specification, as the trim was of the more expensive de luxc level anyway.

That extra 16 horsepower was accompanied by a rise in torque from 44 lb ft. to 55 lb ft., which made the car a very accurate taster for the Mini

A nice picture to tell the story of the 997's new features which included the wire-mesh grille carburettors and three branch large bore exhaust manifold as aids towards 55 bhp. Another important, and widely copied, fitment was the remote control linkage for the gearbox. The small disc brakes did not have a good reputation

Cooper 1275 S of later years. Both cars could be driven in top gear from 15 mph upward, to the accompaniment of initial vibration, but pulling lustily nonetheless. Owing to their low weight which *Motor* measured as $12\frac{1}{2}$ cwt (1400 lb) compared to the 112 lb less they recorded for the 850, both 997 Cooper and the later big-engine S-types were noted for their top gear fleetness. Today the time of 16.5s that the 997 recorded for passing busily in fourth from 50–70 mph would be regarded as slow for an enthusiast's car, but it is still fully 3.5s faster than *Autocar* recorded for 50–70 in top for the 998 Austin Metro of 41 bhp, of 51 lb ft. torque and a tubby 1675 lb in 1981! On the other side of the coin, the Metro achieves 84 to 87 mph, (Cooper 85 to 84 mph in *Motor*) depending on wind direction, this on an alleged 14 horsepower *less* than the Mini Cooper of 20 years previously. As for mpg, *Motor* recorded 34.6 mpg on British

Combustion chamber for Mini-Cooper displays classic heart shape and principles that live on in the eighties effectively

roads that had no overall limit in September 1961 with the 997 Cooper, while *Autocar* managed only 35.2 mpg in the economy-biased basic Metro of 1981.

However a constant speed comparison again says a lot about the power needed to propel a Mini, any original shape Mini, through the air. At a constant 30 mph, 56.5 mpg for a 1961 Mini-Cooper, and for the 1981 Mini-Metro? A convincing 67.4 mpg. At higher speed, constant 80 mph in each case, those 20-year-apart *Motor* and *Autocar* test results show 29 mpg for the Metro and 27 for Mini-Cooper 997! That is two mpg constant-speed progress, and less than 1 mpg overall at face values in twenty years. Perhaps the basic Mini philosophy of light weight was more important than today's emphasis on better equipped, and

The 1961 Mini-Cooper disc was a less capable unit than was later possible for the wider-wheeled Cooper S models

Torture chamber! BMC were not about to cosset early sixties customers with refinements like reclining seat backs. However you got the efficient remote gearchange and the supplementary instrumentation of de luxe models. The throttle pedal must hold some sort of record for Miniscule dimensions

therefore heavier, aerodynamically-conscious designs?

Other improvements

The revised lower three ratios, and the engine's extended rpm range allowed BMC to offer 28 mph, 45 and 65 mph as recommended gearchange points on the central speedometer: no tachometer was ever offered as standard on either Cooper or Cooper S models, but few ran many miles before getting that and the many other 'standard' Mini

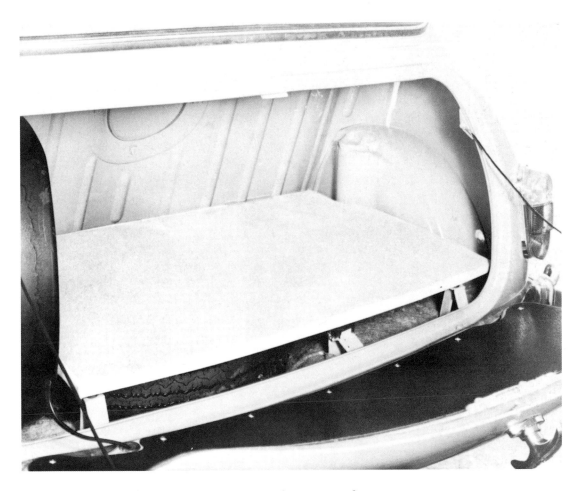

tweaks which apparently every enthusiast adopted.

As in the case of the basic Mini, the 997 Cooper was a tuner's paradise, though some of the ideas, notably the adoption of simple remote control linkage for the Cooper gearchange looked as though they might take bread and butter work from the ever-multiplying Mini accessory makers. In fact that remote change idea was successfully offered for years by SPQR, its sales seemingly enhanced by the Cooper image, and you could still

The refinement of a boot floor was to be found in Coopers, the spare wheel beneath

31

sell a Cooper owner anything from further tuning — Daniel Richmond of Downton soon sprinted a road going 997 to the other side of the then-magic 'ton', 100 mph — to a small rim steering wheel, initially in wood, but later likely to be real or imitation leather.

In short, despite the Cooper derivatives, the Mini's now incredibly basic trim, pre-dating even the Japanese assault on the motorcycle industry, never mind their comprehensively equipped cars, was a dream to the infant conversions business. The extra power of the Cooper derivatives, particularly the later big-engined models, meant that a lot more extra weight, in the form of some early hatchback coachwork, or plush leather trims and Rolls-Royce paint and woodwork standards, could be carried around by specialist versions of the now almost unrecognisable 'people's car.'

The 997 Cooper also offered disc brakes. I rarely drove either the later 998 or 997 with any but non-standard brakes, so I assume that some of the comment about the limited usefulness of the tiny 7 in. diameter Lockheed discs and associated small calipers must have been justified. Yet, a glance at the Abingdon built specifications for their works cars, contained in Peter Browning's *The Works Minis,* shows that they used to fit DS11s and VG95s for the rear shoes (themselves unchanged over the 850s and scarcely needed on a car with over 60 per cent of its distributed weight up front), use Lockheed Heavy Duty fluid and that was it, aside from the precaution of running brake lines inside the car out of the way of rocks and the like.

When you consider that 'the rally cars produced around 70 bhp,' according to Peter, and were capable of winning genuine international rallies for the brief season they enjoyed pre-

Cooper S, those maligned little anchors did a gallant job. However, they were improved during the production run (March 1963) and the Cooper S used a different, and larger, front disc arrangement.

Austin Cooper leads Morris on the original launch testing session for journalists, the leading car already minus a hubcap

Otherwise the basic Cooper concept of a now available Super trim level—easily identified by gauges either side of the speedometer, ignition key starting instead of the original floor button and opening rear windows—combined to the mechanical changes described, remained in production until January 1964.

In its short competition lifespan (effectively 1962) it had taken the BRSCC's forerunner to the British Saloon Car Championship for South

In action the 997 proved comparatively economical as well as able to reach 85 mph in production trim. Today its performance can be found, or exceeded in normal family cars, but not its unique blend of cheerful charm, and an amazing ability to scuttle from point A to B in the minimum time necessary to put an enormous grin on a driver's face

African John Love in the John Cooper-run example, and took nine class wins (two outright) in the European Championship. Works 997s did run on into 1963—Rauno Aaltonen managing a remarkable third overall on that year's Monte— but more of that, and other Mini-Cooper exploits in the chapters devoted to their racing and rallying achievements.

Meantime, it could be seen that the 997 Mini-Cooper, whether badged by Austin or Morris, had achieved its objectives. There was now a distinct awe surrounding the Mini's competition achievements against inevitably bigger cars, while the road Coopers darted their way from the factories at a brisk 750 a week on peak demand. That's about the levels they're talking of for all Minis in the wake of Metro!

Altogether approximately 25,000 Mini-Cooper 997s were made. Good going for a car that was originally slated for a production trial run of 1000 copies, anticipated at a possible 25 a week in early talks!

Chapter 3
998: overlooked and forgotten

The 998 derivative of the original 997 upsets our chronology on a yearly basis—the 1071 Cooper S pre-dated it by nearly a year—but it was so closely allied to the 997, outside its sweeter and shorter stroke 9FA/998 motor, that it demands to be placed immediately after that model.

The 998 is the acid test of how you love Coopers today. If you are looking for an investment, the 998 seems a poorer bet than the Coopers that sandwich its January 1964–November 1969 production life—a life that brought total Cooper production to 101,242 examples. That is over double the S-type total and, even though over 50 per cent were exported, there should still be more good examples more readily available than there are of the more glamorous S, a model which sold three times as many units overseas as it did inside the UK!

Working against the 998 as an investment is the fact that the factory never used it as a competition car. They had no need. The 997 did the rally and racing job for 1962 and the months of 1963 that preceded homologation of the vastly superior (for competition) 1071 S.

So you may find a 998 with an interesting history, but there is not a factory one that I can trace. Yet the 998 has more merit as a road car than is likely to be remembered today.

Blenheim seems as good place as any for two girls to get stuck in a Mini-Cooper. More interesting for fashion writers than Cooper owners as this 1963 probable 997 sits on its C41 crossplies. Outwardly the 998 looked the same . . .

Testing both 1275 S and 998 basic production models in the August 1967 issue of *Cars & Car Conversions*, Martyn Watkins felt, 'in standard form, however, they are both sporting little cars, with good roadholding and admirable performance, although when ultimate top speed and acceleration are not of vital importance we would be inclined to settle for the Cooper 998 (a D-registered 1966 example) as a road car. Because, although it doesn't do quite so much, it does what it does do in a pleasanter fashion.'

To the author's mind the opinion of Martyn Watkins was important, and more relevant, than any number of contemporary road tests or my own memories, because M. B. Watkins had probably driven more Mini examples than anyone of the period. Why? *Cars & Car Conversions* literally took off on the strength of the Mini tuning boom. The staff got sick of the subject towards the end,

and successfully anticipated the Escort takeover, but when I joined *C & CC* (September 1967) there was still an awful lot of Mini mileage to be done, aside from that in my own converted 850.

During nearly six years' production, over twice the run of the 997, there were a number of important changes to the 998, changes that we list in our appendix. Important at the time was the introduction of Dunlop SP41 radials (or the India 'badged' equivalent), but any example you find today would be likely to have some other type of radial fitted. Compared with the original crossply equipment, I remember the biggest change as being the speed of response in turning into a corner, and a noticeable bonus in grip with a welcome increase in tyre life. A teenage gorilla like myself in the sixties could reduce the old C41s to molten canvas in 6000 hectic road miles, whereas the same rugged treatment on the tuned car

BMC did their best to link Cooper racing cars and the road Mini-Coopers. The author thinks this might be Goodwood and observes the skilful brushwork that has emphasised the Austin Cooper badge on the bonnet with interest

37

Dunlop SP3 tyre was made in Germany and its chunky looks were as fashionable on sixties' Minis as Pirelli P7s are on eighties' Porsches. The SP3 and SP41 tyres were critical to Cooper development

Dunlop SP41 tyre also had an India-branded equivalent and was a lot more durable than both SP3 and C41

provided over 10,000 miles, even if the front SPs were left *in situ* throughout their life.

Of more mechanical moment in production changes was the adoption of Hydrolastic suspension in September 1964, and an incredible four years later they saw fit to let us have the synchromesh on first gear that had been a grizzle throughout the sixties. The Hydrolastic suspension was not well-loved—even on a 998 it allowed large differences in attitude between braking and acceleration.

Yet, according to the best retrospective information I can find, Mini-Cooper kept Hydrolastic, unaltered, to the end of its life, while the S-type had stiffer settings in 1966 and the ordinary Minis dropped the system, reverting to the rubber cones, in October 1968.

A better engine

If you want to run a Cooper today, the 998 also offers the bonus of an engine that is basically still in production, albeit in single carburettor, 39 bhp, power trim for 1981 Minis. Even in the eighties the bore and stroke remained unaltered at 64.58 mm by 76.20 mm. That is still slightly under-square, of course, but it was a much smoother engine for road, and track, use than the 5.08 mm longer stroke 997.

The basic construction also differed over the 997 in that the pistons had raised crowns—ratios of 9:1 or 7.8:1 with consequent power differences were offered during production, but few low compression models ever found their way into UK dealerships.

Another fundamental engine change over the 997 was the adoption of floating small ends. Instead of the 997's clamp bolts to retain gudgeon pins, there was a press fitting to the top end of the connecting rods, retained by circlips that were

The Mini-Cooper was tres chic *to the French and contributed a lot of goodwill toward BMC that lasted Leyland well until the eighties' launch of Metro*

This SP3-shod Cooper looks a bit over the top while resting at the Cowley export department. Look at those ornate wheel trims and headlamp chrome cowlings, never mind the wickerwork popularised when Peter Sellers adopted it

grooved to fit within the pistons. Clive Trickey said of its power potential at the time, 'this engine is very much stronger, and more reliable, than the old longer-stroke model.'

Aside from the continued use of a crankshaft damper—which was perhaps more to reassure the owner that something was being done to keep 6500 rpm as a reasonably safe limit on this three bearing four cylinder—the Cooper 998 used a different cylinder head, pistons and camshaft to the 998 Wolseley Hornet/Riley Elf. The latter had pre-dated the Cooper 998 by arriving on the market in November 1962, with an advertised 38 bhp and 52 lb ft. torque in single SU, 8.3:1 compression ratio specification.

The 998 Cooper was fitted with the same twin $1\frac{1}{4}$ in. SU carburettors and three branch exhaust system that the 997s employed, but the camshaft and valves were different. The cam was a 0.312 lift action again, but duration was that of normal Minis (230 degree) on a shaft coded AEA 630 as against 997 Cooper's 2A 948 of 22 degree duration. Perhaps as compensation, the 998 offered larger inlet valves, measuring 1.219 in. inlet and 1 in. exhaust compared to the same size exhaust and 1.156 inlet for 997.

Horsepower and torque figures reflected the subtle changes in the engine's breathing characteristics, and the change in stroke/bore ratio. Maximum power was still quoted at 55 bhp, but at 200 rpm less than on the 997. Torque value was fractionally up at 57 lb ft. for the 998, again at reduced (minus 600 revs) rpm, the peak for 998 at 3000 rpm.

Cooper detail modifications that carried over from the 997 included the 70 lb release point for the oil pressure pump spring in the release valve and the use of a 9 lb pressure release radiator cap.

And now . . . the bad news

With the yardstick of the Cooper S to draw upon, the 998 was generally slated over its braking performance with the original 997 Cooper front discs. Little could be done, because the Cooper didn't have the wider, ventilated, $4\frac{1}{2}$ in. rims that came on Cooper S's, so there was not the space to accommodate that model's superior equipment. It could be done today, but would involve a comprehensive conversion employing a large number of S-type, or possible 1275 GT parts (remembering that the 1275 GT went over to 12 in. wheels during the late seventies) and might not appeal to those who want their cars to feel as well as look original!

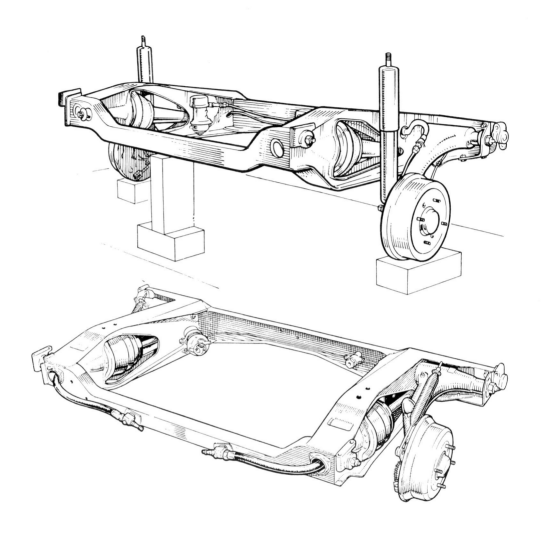

Top the more popular 'dry' or rubber cone back suspension layout.

Below the Hydrolastic or 'wet' system with pressure adjustment valves clearly visible at the rear of the subframe

How did those brakes feel? Once again Mini-maestro Watkins was on top of the situation, one that had been little improved by the early dispensation of the so called 'brake intensifier' (a crude servo) early in the life of 997. Watkins said of the 998, 'the biggest disadvantage on the 998 Cooper raises its ugly head when you come to stopping the beast. The seven inch disc brakes

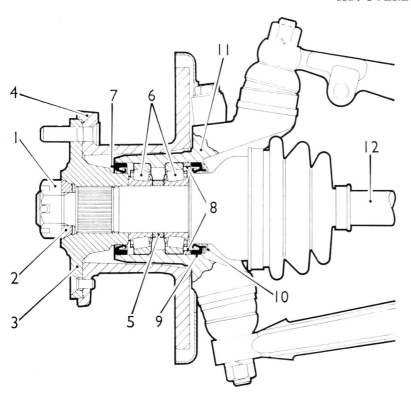

1. Drive shaft nut.
2. Outer tapered collar.
3. Driving flange.
4. Hub and disc assembly.
5. Bearing distance ring.
6. Taper roller bearings.
7. Outer oil seal.
8. Spacer (inner bearing to seal).
9. Inner oil seal.
10. Water shield.
11. Swivel hub.
12. Drive shaft.

Mini-Cooper hub and disc detail

are, admittedly, better than those fitted to early Coopers—they needed to be—but they still provide remarkably little stopping for remarkably high pressure. So long as you don't overdo it, however, they will stop the car. But if you use 'em too much, too often, they fade right away. And fast driving, where other traffic is, has to be an exercise in thinking ahead if your pride and joy isn't going to end up with a short wheelbase.' *C & CC* may not have been the delight of English scholars, but they knew an impending accident when they drove one!

All the usual Mini problems—poor driving position on a plastic-covered park bench, switchgear that could not be reached, and noise—were present on 998, but it still collected press praise.

Above *late production (October 1968) Mini-Cooper 998 in the Mk II body. The sliding windows remain but the larger rear lamps and simplified grille shape are obvious, as are the SP41 radials*

Right *another one for students of fashion and social habits. The Mk II-bodied 998 Cooper waits to show its 80 mph paces to the young man who has forsaken Cooper jollity for the joys of consulting the young lady about the absence of an engine for this craft. Or perhaps it is her car and she is going to tow him to eternity? Anyway the Cooper looks nice in two tone paint...*

To my mind it also signalled the end of the conventional mass production sports car as a convincing alternative to the sports saloon. The 1275 cc Mk III Sprite was priced in the same £660–£700 league in 1967, but the Cooper image was sportier, a little more frugal, and more relevant to the kind of motor club member who likes to get out there in the action. It was more likely that such a man would buy the more expensive, and effective, Cooper S; but if he was stuck on a budget there were plenty of bits he could add to the Mini in stages.

When people ask me 'what happened to the mass production sports car?' I reply that it died with the original small-bumper Spridgets and MGBs: the TR7 never qualified, and the Mini-Cooper was the model that showed people a four seater could be more fun, more practical and more effective in motor sport.

Chapter 4
S-type revolution begins: 1071 S

In casual conversation, the subject of the Mini-Cooper S-types usually arouses memories of the biggest capacity derivative, 1275 S. The 'twelve seven five' had the longest production run (1964–mid 1971); the longest list of outright race and rally successes at the highest levels (though the 1071 took one of the S-type's three official Monte wins); and by far the biggest percentage of Cooper S production, which totalled 44,859 of these ultimate production-line examples of the fast Mini.

Yet the 1071 S was announced before the 1275 (March 1963—1071), and took a very serious international first-time victory for the Abingdon factory team (Alpine, Rauno Aaltonen, June 1963). The 1071 S may not be so well remembered in the eighties, but this charming blend between 1275 lugging power and the 970's high rpm capabilities, brought home a lot of rally-winning

Authentic 1965 bonnet badge is on left with 1966 Morris equivalent (right)

bacon in nine months of general use that preceded the 1275. It won the Alpine and Monte, producing a popular win for Paddy Hopkirk on the latter, as well as a third overall on the 1963 Tour de France and fourth on the same year's RAC Rally.

So it was as good a competition car as you would expect, given the potential exhibited by the 997 Mini Cooper, but what made BMC build such a little hot rod anyway?

A month after the original 997 Cooper announcement in 1961, Stuart Turner, then a youthful and even more aggressive 27 years of age, became Abingdon's competitions manager. As the team progressed with Turner weeding out some gentlemen amateurs in favour of professionals on the driving side, and getting respect from the first class team of mechanics that his predecessor Marcus Chambers had gathered, it was inevitable that the demand for a quicker Mini derivative would grow. Much the same applied to the works-backed racing Coopers: the potential was clearly there in the Mini's still-astonishing cornering for an extra dose of straightline speed.

Given the brick-like shape of the car, there was only one answer—more power! And, given due acknowledgement to the part played in the success of all A-series engines to the Weslake-patented areas of combustion, there was only one engineering outfit to show how that power could be augmented reliably for the road, and substantially for competition: Daniel Richmond's at Downton. Richmond's developed 997 Cooper was soon being studied at Longbridge, and a firm decision was taken in the winter of 1962/63 to go ahead to build officially at least the 1000 needed for Group 2 competition acceptance. It seems that, even when putting the 1071 engined derivative of S into production—at an eventual selling price of £695 7s 7d because then-Chancellor

Reginald Maudling had actually *reduced* Purchase Tax—they had both 1275 and 970 S-derivatives in mind, these being little more than stroke alterations on the fundamentally redesigned S-engine anyway.

S-types engine engineering

Again BMC were not content merely to tweak up existing power plant, rather offering a complete rethink of their original 997 offering.

True, the 68.26 mm stroke of the 1071 S was the

Inside a 1275 S, showing the more conventional air cleaners adopted (compared to early Cooper) and the brake servo-assistance. They had to take off the wiper arms to gain a little more access for this picture, which also displays the underbonnet sound proofing

A bonus in frictional area offered by the S-type larger rimmed 10 in diameter wheels provided a disproportionate improvement in braking, which became excellent by the standards of the day, thanks to the larger discs that could be accommodated

The Swiss took the Mini-Cooper S too. In fact, Swiss former GP driver Clay Regazzoni learned some of his craft in such a car

Mini-Cooper S scuttles past the Longbridge plant design office

same as for original 848 Mini, but that was one of few fundamental links between the original and the S-types. The principles of ADO15 were left untouched in this ADO50 (Mini Cooper) evolution, but myriad details constantly rearranged themselves.

At the heart of this ultimate-performance edition of the production engine was the crankshaft. Nitrided by Rolls-Royce, no less, we were assured at the time, and very different, even to a 997. At 1071 cc the dimensions were 70.6 mm × 68.26 mm, which meant bringing the centre

cylinders closer together by a quarter inch—*but* the overall gap between cylinders was increased. This offset of the centre lines was accommodated by a fractional reduction in main bearing widths (again three supported the crankshaft), and a substantial increase in bearing surface area through a quarter inch increase in bearing diameter (a solid 2 in. total diameter). This meant offsetting the small end, and thus redesigning the connecting rods, which incorporated a nearly one-inch increase in diameter and a rather more rugged piston pin design.

Cooper S was also used as plain clothes police car in the sixties

Original series Cooper S today in mid-restoration phase. The car is identified as a 1964 by our researcher, but carries the 1966 D-registration plate. It also displays the almost inevitable rust of the exterior rear seams

Lubrication was not neglected on the Type 10F 1071 S motor either; a 75 psi pressure point was selected for the relief spring and that pressure constantly maintained according to the toughest of contemporary road tests. Oil galleries were enlarged, and the pump itself drew on Formula Junior and early Formula 3 experience.

Again valve sizes went up, in fact to 1.406 in. inlet and 1.219 in. exhaust, but it was the materials that drew comment. For the use of Nimonic 80 steels, welded stellite tips and guides formed in Hidural 5 copper nickel alloys all made good copy.

Camshaft timing was quite mild for the road versions. The S shaft, shared between all three models of the time, was the 998's, (coded AEA 630) having the same kind of lift as a Cooper 997, but for competition the classic 649 (the 648 was also the same profile) shaft, served well. Not only in Minis, for it was later substantially the same in its valve gear demands when employed inside some Ford competition engines—and doubtless many others whose makers did not reveal the origins of their vigorous camming!

In production form, the head seems to have suffered initially from overheating, later alevitated as 1275 production encountered these problems. In 1071 S form compression was 9:1 and the HS2 twin SU carburettors of $1\frac{1}{4}$ in. bore were retained. This was sufficient to allow 70 bhp at 6000 rpm (up 15 bhp over Cooper) and 62 lb ft. of torque at 4500 rpm. Some 1500 revs up the scale

A good look at the underbonnet layout of a 1969 Mk II 1275 S shows detail changes to standard specification from a private owner. The engine is most remembered for lusty torque and rather rougher operation than its smaller brethren

on a 998 Cooper, but with a bonus of 5 lb ft. extra torque as some compensation.

Naturally the 1071 S was quicker, but it was to the credit of BMC, and of Issigonis as head of the conceptual Mini team of experts that they did something about the brakes and handling. Thus the famous $4\frac{1}{2}$ in. rim, but still 10 in. diameter, steel S-type wheels replaced the $3\frac{1}{2}$ in. wide units of the Mini 850/997 or 998 Cooper. The extra width not only allowing a little extra tyre section to meet the road (Dunlop 5.50 SPs were found on the test cars instead of 5.20 C41 or SP of lesser models) but also a bigger front disc area.

Correct rear end regalia from the Mk II Mini-Cooper 1275 S of 1967/68. This example also has the status of the twin tanks that began as an option and became standard in later models

Left another twist to the badging and a Mk II face for Cooper S

59

The factory captioned this 'the legendary Mini-Cooper S shown here in Mk II form, 1967.' Fair enough, but note how the two tone paint is not obligatory, that the wheels are plainer in appearance with a non-white finish and simple hubcaps to replace the earlier ornate ones that Coopers shared with other Minis of the period. No longer is it possible to tell at a glance between Austin and Morris versions using the grille as a guide; the badges have to do the trick with the adoption of broader slats on Austin as well as Morris

Offsetting—a fashionable word today, but in connection with front suspension geometry—the one inch wide wheels relative to the Cooper S discs allowed increased airflow (the wheels were ventilated anyway), and room for an extra half inch disc diameter ($7\frac{1}{2}$ in. total) and an eighth of an inch on thickness. The still sorely missed, Laurence Pomeroy calculated this as providing a 'mass of metal available as a heat sink increased by 80 per cent.'

Naturally the area swept by the front pads was enlarged, providing a total of 20 extra inches of swept area and the specification of the pad material itself was biased towards fighting fade rather than cold response. Servo assistance, through a Lockheed $5\frac{1}{2}$ in. diameter Hydrovac unit, was standard from the beginning.

Other changes for the S, introduced with the 1071, included needle roller bearings for the gearbox, bonded clutch linings and double spring operation for the diaphragm unit.

Suspension: wet or dry?

Today we might find it surprising that so little was changed on the roadholding side—bearing in mind the catalogue of modifications that even agile cars like the VW Golf and front drive Ford Escort go through before they emerge in performance in GTI or XR3 trim. Yet there was only one very significant suspension production change during the Mini-Cooper S type's life, more applicable to the 1275 than the 1071 S.

In September 1964, two months after the 1071 S was officially discontinued, the fluid-and-air-pressurised system Hydrolastic was introduced to Cooper models, a move shared on all Mini saloons. During April/May 1966 a stiffer action Hydrolastic was offered in an attempt to cut down some of the fore and aft pitch referred to in the 998 chapter, a characteristic that was exaggerated by extra power.

Thus many high performance Minis, competition-destined, or otherwise, reverted to rubber suspension.

Authentic badge looks like a fake but tells the Mk II story

Officially a 1071 S should come on the dry suspension preceding Hydrolastic. The combination of 92 mph, 23–36 mpg (25.8 mpg average) and 0–60 mph timed on their fifth wheel at 11.9s caused *Motoring News* to declare in their 20 June, 1963 issue, 'the last word in small, hot cars. Mini Cooper S—a fast, good handling sports saloon for under £700.'

Motor reported 26.8 mpg overall, 7.8 mpg worse than they had returned on the 997 Mini Cooper, and gave a 0–60 mph figure at 12.9 sec. allied to a best of 98.9 mph (94.5 mph, mean). They commented, 'these are remarkable figures for an 1100 cc saloon capable of seating four people in comfort.'

What I think they meant was that the Mini's ratio of interior space to overall length was remarkable. At still only fractionally over 10 foot, it was perfectly capable of accommodating four. Indeed I used to carry five on visits to Brands Hatch motorcycle meetings of the early sixties— but I would dispute the use of the word 'comfort'!

In fact the grouches, Cooper, or stock Mini, were much the same. Those upright seats, awkward and large steering wheel and switchgear were seemingly located for the exclusive use of the Jolly Green Giant.

Proprietary parts—bucket seats, small sports steering wheels the almost mandatory use of extensions to the switchgear and brackets to lower the steering column, alleviated these problems. The Silent Travel concern (still trading, but under Paddy Hopkirk's ownership these days) attacked the worst problem of the lot; the noise made by an engine close to the bulkhead, allied to all those transfer gears whirring round in sympathy with the kind of energetic driving that was the hallmark of a sizeable percentage of Mini-Madmen.

Enter: biggest S and smallest S

Still the BMC management were not satisfied with the extraordinary growth of their baby. By the close of 1963 production they had made almost exactly threequarters of a million Minis (746,285), and the augmented S-type range brought them untold prestige and competition publicity help in making a million by 1965.

Simply put, the 970 was a very limited-production, homologation special to give competitors a hot runner in the 1-litre saloon car class for racing or rallying. It succeeded brilliantly, and for far longer than its limited production span! The 970 S meant that the usual S-type 70.64 mm bore was allied to an unusually abbreviated, stroke of 61.91 mm. The 1071 brought things

Only the 1275 S made into the seventies with the concealed hinge updated body (Mk III). The car was also assembled from KD kits in Australia after production had ceased in Britain. This one has been tastefully modified with Minilites and flared arches

nearly oversquare at 68.26 mm and the 1275, introduced with the 970 S in March 1964, had a comfortably long stroke of 81.33 mm.

For the road all used the $1\frac{1}{4}$ in. bore SUs, but compression varied between the 9:1 of the 1071 S and the 1275 S's 9.5:1 to the highest production Mini figure of 9.75:1, a ratio that could well be seen again if current fuel efficient high compression fashion is followed to its logical conclusion on the more mundane Minis of the eighties.

The 970 was rated at 65 bhp, with the ordinary Mini-Cooper torque figure of 55 lb ft. (at a highish 6500 and 3500 rpm respectively). But the 1275's roadgoing popularity could easily be explained by more horsepower, 75, more easily reached (5800 rpm), to the accompaniment of truly entrancing torque for a 1.3 litre of 80 lb ft. on 3000 revs—its effect exaggerated by the all up weight of little more than the original Cooper.

To put that figure in an eighties perspective, scan an *Autocar* Buyers Guide and you will soon feel what that meant in such a light and compact car. For instance a 1588 cc Audi ohc motor in low tune produces only 3 lb ft. more; the Allegro 1.5 ohc (nee Maxi) has the same as the Audi, while the present Leyland 1.3 offers 7 lb *less*, the Alfasud 1.35 sohc-per-bank boxer engine has 3 lb ft. less torque and 79bhp at the same rpm . . . and it's ten years since the twin carburettor 1275 S expired, killed by high overheads and low production. Of course, Alfa do offer a Ti model with an advertised 86 bhp and 87 lb ft. torque from 1351 cc, but it does have to propel 1951 lb instead of approximately 1300 lb. The Italian car is, however, undeniably a sleeker object to propel through the air than any Mini.

Short-lived 970 production but. . . .

The 970 S may have only been in production a

Above *Pretty and boxy Mini Cooper. This one's a 970 S of 1965 vintage. Looks clean but not concours. No one could resist chasing that big 'S' badge on the boot lid at the time*

Left *There used to be a passion to show off rally winning cars still with the mud and grime stuck on. Not so this Cooper S, the 1967 Monte Carlo winner now in BL Heritage's museum at Syon Park*

Left *No one who witnessed
John Rhodes and John
Fitzpatrick dicing their way
through the British Saloon
Car Championship will ever
forget this typical pose. Mid-
sixties works Cooper S 1275
versus Broadspeed Ford
Anglia*

Above *The Mark II
bodyshell brought a shade
more refinement to all the
Minis. This one's a well
looked after 998 Cooper of
1968 with popular but non-
standard wider wheels*

Above *Smart Cooper 998 Mk II in replica Cooper racing colours*

Right *Still with external hinges and sliding windows this is a carefully restored Mk II 1275 S from 1970. Wheels, sunroof, door mirror and bonnet catch all non-stock, but desirable*

Far Right *A 1970 Mini Cooper S Mk II on the track 10 years later. A virtually standard car except for the attractive Minilites and seemingly obligatory sunroof*

Above *'As the factory made them' Coopers are very, very rare. Even this 1972 Mk III Cooper S 1275 has been slightly modified*

Right *Still undergoing restoration this is the 1275 S underbonnet sight close to being factory fresh. Bodyshell is Mk III*

Far Right *Some would say the best of them all. Rarity, at least in right hand drive form, makes this Innocenti Mini Cooper 1300 rather special, whatever*

Will the legend live on? Many hope that the Metro Cooper will fill the gap in the 1980s. Although developed by John Cooper and his son it is unlikely that the Cooper badge will grace BL's production version. Performance is up to expectation, so is economy

Roger J. Hill from Essex allowed us this picture of his J-plated Mk III Mini-Cooper 1275 S. Wider wheels and a diminutive Leyland badge are interesting points, the Mk III chiefly identified by the lack of exterior hinges to the leading edge of the doors

short while according to official records—March 1964 to January 1965—but the sporting effect of the 1-litre S lived on. In one of those anomalies that are bound to occur when people start digging into factory competition records, I found that the 970 S (407 ARX) made its Abingdon international competition debut in November *1963*, when Logan Morrison and his journalist co-driver Ross Finlay won their class in the RAC Rally, finishing 19th overall. Production was not listed until March 1964....

The 970 was then occasionally used as a 'class award' car—Tony Fall actually won the August 1966 Polish Rally in a 970 S, and beat Makinen's 1275—in works rally outings, but its real use was saloon car racing.

John Handley exploited the 970, actually running his car as a 999 with approximately 100 bhp, in the European Touring Car Championship. The British Vita machine (KDK 320F) racked up more points than any rival and the lesson was

This tastefully modernised Mk III Mini-Cooper S poses outside Hampton Court, the cleanly extended wheelarches and the Minilite wheels a reminder of the way a lot of Minis were equipped in 1275 S trim

learnt in Britain. Jim Whitehouse at Arden Conversions Ltd, Solihull, put his long-standing Mini racing expertise behind Alec Poole (rather better known for his Spridget exploits), and the result was a win in the 1969 British Saloon Car Championship. That Arden motor was alloy-headed, fuel-injected (Tecalemit-Jackson) and gave 112.5 bhp at some 9500 rpm: less that Arden claimed for the normal race specification 1293 cc S with siamesed port head and single Weber 45DCOE carburettor.

The 1275 S: Character Cooper

So the one litre S gave the Mini's parents something to boast about until the seventies, but what of 1275, what kind of car was that? Avail-

able, in a word! For a start you could always buy one, not always the case with its smaller brothers! Introduced at £778, and costing £849 when it went into Mk II twin-tank guise in 1968, the 1275 S was the ideal choice for a practical road car amongst the S-types. The pulling power can be judged from my earlier comments and the figures in our chart, but to drive one between a modest 40 mph and a nerve tingling 90 mph in fourth (top speed was almost exactly 100 mph, such was the penalty of the shape!) was, and still is, an enjoyable and unique experience.

The kart-like steering, just 2½ turns lock to lock, the *Mini*scule size, and roadholding that was then unmatched—and which will still make you grin broadly, was an attractive combination.

Extensively modified 1969 Mk II Mini-Cooper S with interior rollover bar, full safety harness for driver, electric window operation and the more usual Minilite/wheelarch extension conversion

Rare Minibird. A 1974 right-hand drive Innocenti Mini-Cooper S-based 1300

Then add an overall 28.5 mpg from *Motoring News* in 1968; 26.8 mpg from the same outfit in 1965, and 27–28 mpg in my own hands (1969) and you see the attractions. Advantages which are probably more relevant in today's traffic jams and escalating petrol prices than they were in the comparatively benign sixties.

Snags? On the 1275 in particular there was a definite engine roughness that you traded for all the long stroke pulling prowess. Otherwise there was the usual gear lever sizzle when approaching maximum gear speeds of little over 30 mph in first, 55 in second and 80 mph in third. Anything much over 80 mph, which could be reached in some 20 sec. from a standstill, was thus the point at which

rapid acceleration tailed off, and the motor started getting rougher in top gear too. Over 90 mph you did wonder if it could possibly stay together another second longer, but it usually did, though at the penalty of some fairly high indicated water temperatures, if the punishment was kept up. Instrumentation was the usual Super de Luxe, and they never did get round to offering a tachometer, though you could purchase seats with reclining backrests for £15 as an option by 1968!

In the production life of the 1275 S the most important milestones were: Hydrolastic suspension in the year of introduction; the reclining seat option in late 1965; twin petrol tanks (from $5\frac{1}{2}$ to

From the side the Innocenti Mini-Cooper 1300 displays unique production wheels and opening front quarter vents, plus front wing repeater flashers. Interiors of the Innocenti Minis were always reckoned to be far superior to the British product—and there was an alternative external body from the Italians too

77

11 gallons) and an oil cooler in early 1966; the high rate Hydrolastic, accompanied by solid universals for the inboard end of the driveshafts in spring 1966; autumn 1967's Mk II—which was meant to have an all-synchromesh gearbox, but didn't (even on press cars!) for complete production fitment until the following year!

A Mk III, based on the ADO20 Mini shell with concealed door hinges, wind-up windows and clubman door trims was made in limited numbers through 1970 to the summer of 1971, when July saw BL's most gallant giant killer of all time murdered in its turn by a management who had the brass neck to offer the 1275 GT in its place. Not a bad Mini, but not a thoroughbred in the S-mould.

So, with the whirring of a thousand gears, the threshing of side-radiatored, three bearing motor, and the scrabble of tiny tyres fresh in our minds, let's see how the Minis stacked up against each other in figures.

	848	997	998	1971 S	970 S	1275 S
Bore × stroke (mm)	62.94 ×68.26	62.43 ×81.28	64.58 ×76.20	70.64 ×68.26	70.64 ×61.91	70.64 ×81.33
Peak power (bhp)	34	55	55	70	65	76
Max torque (lb ft.)	44	54	57	62	55	79
Top speed (mph)	72	85	86	92	89	99
0–60 mph (seconds)	25	17.2	14.8	12.5	–	11
Overall mpg	42	35	33	27	–	26
Produced	1959–80	1961–64	1964–69	1963–64	1964–65	1964–71
Price at intro. (£)	497	679	675	695	–	778
Tyres (R=Radial)	5.20	5.20	145(R)	145(R)	145(R)	145(R)
Mph per 1000 rpm	14.85	14.85	14.7	14.7	14.7	16.05
Wheels (inches)	3.5 × 10	3.5 × 10	3.5 × 10	4.5 × 10	4.5 × 10	4.5 × 10
Suspension type	Rubber or Hydrolastic	Rubber	Rubber then Hydrolastic	Rubber	Rubber	Hydro-lastic
Front brakes (rears all 7 in. drum)	Drum, 7 in.	Disc, 7.0	Disc, 7.0	Disc, 7.5	Disc, 7.5	Disc, 7.5

Chapter 5
Saloon car racing's smallest

Goodwood, Crystal Palace, Brands Hatch: those were the venues where I began to watch motor racing in the mid-sixties. Armed with my NUJ press card from my work at IPC Business Press (*Poultry Farmer* was intensely interested in motor racing, and had been known for years of regular attendance at motorcycle meetings before that!) I stood and watched race programmes that offered a lot for the 50p I occasionally had to pay when my farming press card failed to impress . . . Jim Clark, Graham Hill, Jacky Ickx and many more topliners would then race Formula 2 machinery, saloons and sports cars during one meeting. Mighty good value.

Looking back over 22 years it seems as though, when the Mini was born out of the Issigonis/Lord marriage of design and production genius, it took to the track straight away. Almost six years of Mini racing development had preceded the spectacle that met my eyes as an astonished spectator.

I thought I drove my little tuned up 850 fast, though it seemed dreadfully underpowered compared with the 650 cc Triumph Bonneville motorcycle that preceded it. Then I saw these track Minis fighting Ford Anglias that were like no other Anglias I had ever seen. When they added two-wheeling Cortinas and rumbling Mustangs

Paddy Hopkirk finished a fine third on the 1963 Tour de France with 33EJB, in 1071 S form. The same registration and cubic capacity Mini also won the 1964 Monte Carlo Rally. Here the car negotiates a tarmac competitive section with the aid of Henry Liddon

and Falcons, it was all too much. I became a saloon car racing freak, and determined to get a job where I could write about such things, and drive them.

That objective was achieved in 1967; and I have followed Mini fortunes with professional respect ever since. 'Respect' because it is the only car that has spanned 1959 (hitting the headlines in 1960 with a celebrity race that included Jim Clark and John Surtees in 850s) to the 'eighties with tremendous success. There simply is no other car that has enjoyed such saloon success, proving the basic qualities that the Issigonis integrity of principle provided from the start. Of course there have been lean periods, and massive changes in the modifications necessary for a Mini to win in a formula where modifications are free, but today's Mini Seven Club restricted formulae and the loyalty of countless club racers all over the world still depend on Mini production principles.

The flavour of saloon car racing twenty years and more ago is sharply revived by this road-registered (and tyred) Mini-Cooper at Silverstone in 1962. Grille and bumper removal were almost mandatory for any would-be racer, but the police hated to see those sharp edges revealed on public roads

April 1965 and the Mini-Cooper S bug has certainly bitten at the Silverstone round of the British saloon car championship. Aside from the striped works S-types there were also entries from Broadspeed, Alexander and many other professional tuning equipes

Because there is such a two-decade racing history, the Mini still initiates many novices to the satisfaction and heartbreak of motor racing. In Britain at least it is the cheapest way to go saloon car racing—and one of the cheapest and most competitive ways of racing in any form.

In the beginning

The original 850s had been raced with some class success before the advent of the 997 Coopers in 1961; yet it was the extra capacity and potential of the Cooper that finally set the Mini off on the road to international success. I have merely extracted some of the international and pres-

tigious British titles that the car has won in my accompanying table. That tale of triumphs extends back to the 1-litre disc-braked Coopers.

Fittingly, it was the Cooper Car Co. with their unforgettable BRG livery allied to distinctive white bonnet stripes, basically the same as Jack Brabham had had on his World Championship cars of 1959–60, that received the most support in the early days.

Working in association with Daniel Richmond, Cooper's Coopers attacked the British Racing and Sports Car Club's (BRSCC) British saloon car championship. This was the forerunner of the RAC-recognised series that officially took over in

Mini-Coopers looked like cleaning up the 1962 saloon supporting race to the Belgian GP at Spa-Francorchamps, but were jumped in the closing stages by the Auto Union two stroke to their right. Problem was that present day Vauxhall expert Bill Blydenstein had lost all but third gear and they were trying to arrange a Mini dead heat 1-2-3

*Mini-Cooper at its factory
racing peak of the mid-
sixties. John Rhodes tackles
the quick corners of
Silverstone with professional
exhuberance*

1968 and which, by the 'eighties, had evolved into the Tricentrol RAC British Saloon Championship.

Cooper employed then Formula 1 aspirant John Love of South Africa, and Sir John Whitmore the racing baronet who has never liked to use his title. Love came home with the Mini's second national title in the UK, for Whitmore had won the 1961 BRSCC title to get the Cooper drive.

The Mini continued with class or outright wins in the British Championship right through the tyre-smoking sensational years of John Rhodes's unique style in the sixties to 1978 and 1979. Then West Country Mini-man extraordinary, Richard Longman, took the outright title in a 1275 GT against the best opposition that Ford and Alfa Romeo could provide in the class. Altogether the Mini has won the British title five times, an unmatched record which is backed by an enormous number of class titles achieved with 997 or 970 (1-litre) and 1275 (1.3-litre) models.

These class wins were achieved by tremendously talented drivers who were often very unlucky not to add to Mini's overall clutch of Championship outright titles. Men like John Rhodes, the supreme Mini spectacle and the fastest Mini man of his era—which was really the 10 in. wheel period. By the time 12 in. wheels were introduced all round, in the 1969 season, to be allied with fuel injection to try and match the increasingly sophisticated Broadspeed Escorts, there were other drivers who were as fast, or on occasions faster, but never so stirring to watch.

One of my fondest saloon car racing memories dates back to that sixties period of illicit spectating. Standing on the old South Bank section of Brands Hatch, a continuous left made up to half a mile by a mid section easing of the curve, I just couldn't believe the things Rhodes could do with a

Mini. It arrived in view like a 100 mph smoke canister bursting from the tarmac. It then rocked past this astounded spectator with the rear wheel over a foot in the air, the wheel gradually losing speed as testimony to the time it had been airborne. The Mini settled onto that rear wheel only briefly before the whole impossible stunt began again for the sharper left onto the Grand Prix Circuit. It won my heart, but it won Rhodes no more than class titles. The quiet and modest John always had to battle against the Ford or Mini opposition. Which could come from Broadspeed in their Mini days (pre-1966) or the Superspeed Broadspeed Anglias (former Mini ace John

Club racing at Brands, a natural Mini habitat from the sixties (shown here) to the present day. Here speedshop proprietor Mac Ross hurls his S type into Druids bend ahead of Brian Cox, who has gone to the trouble of putting the water radiator out in the breeze with the oil cooler

In 1969 Abingdon were forced to go racing themselves against the team they had supported in previous years. Here John Handley's factory 12 in wheeled, fuel injected 1275 Mk II S holds off an even more spectacular Gordon Spice in the Cooper Britax S. Spice later went on to dominate British saloon car races of the seventies with a Ford Capri. Handley went on to own Dealer Opel Team, while the Mini-Cooper S went into racing oblivion following this season, so far as the factory were concerned. The knowledge lived on in different guises in the eighties . . .

Fitzpatrick won the 1966 title in a Broadspeed Anglia) and, in the final, and only direct year of Abingdon's official participation Rhodes found that men like Gordon Spice had now served their apprenticeship and were capable of beating the master. . . . Abingdon had to learn new racing tricks.

Looking back from the eighties, it is possible to see that Abingdon had a really tough task on their plate in 1969. The Escorts were claimed to give 150 bhp and in the hands of Fitzpatrick and Chris Craft there would be nothing given away. Then there was also a rival team of Minis to beat, the disgruntled Cooper Car Co., banished from works favouritism by Lord Stokes's influence, running a team of yellow and black Minis for Spice and Midlands accessory dealer Steve Neal to prove that they could beat the Abingdon men, John

Rhodes and John Handley. . . . It was the first time Abingdon had been asked to compete in this hard fought arena, for rallying was their game, and Mini or Healey the name on their countless international winners.

Yet outright wins became more frequent despite defeat in the 1300 class. As the 1300s robbed each other of points and watched the Escorts frequently disappear in the distance (the Mini was still king in the wet though, thanks to Spice and Handley), the meticulous work of Jim Whitehouse at Arden and the continuous class success of Alec Poole's 112 bhp 1-litre stole the British crown outright for the Mini in 1969, the first time the overall title had been taken since the early sixties.

Other manufacturers played that 1-litre game with even greater success in the seventies. Bill McGovern took an Imp to three titles in a row in the opening years of that decade, while John Buncombe took the 1300 title once (1972), using a Group 2 Longman-prepared 1293 cc Cooper S.

The demise of the Mini in the 1300 class was due to the limits of roadholding and power being reached, the latter despite overboring to 1293 cc and an eight port, fuel injected cylinder head design in use from 1967 onward. Though the gallant A-series engine could be persuaded to give close to 140 bhp, you then had to transmit it to the road. Sure, the 12 in. diameter wheels helped, especially with Dunlop's incredible Grand Prix-style approach to compounding and construction to keep this large scale customer happy (they expended more effort on Mini tyres than on Jackie Stewart's World Championship winning Matra-Cosworth V8 according to then-competition chief Ian Mills!) but there were still substantial power losses imposed by the Mini's gear train.

Paul Harmer, a later Brands Hatch press officer, at work in a typical 1972 modified club racing Mini, complete with glassfibre front end at the Mallory Park track

Club racers, unbound by tight legislation, resorted to still more power and yet bigger tyres, allied to lightweight space frame construction to keep the little brick right in the forefront of battle during the seventies. Power units got more and more sophisticated, starting with the adaption of the Cosworth SCA (Single Cam A-series) to the Mini transmission and extending as routine, by the eighties, to 1.3-litre Minis rated at 175 bhp and beyond, thanks to DOHC, 16-valve adaptations of the Ford Cosworth BDA motor.

Unwittingly, the backing British Leyland put behind the one marque formula for the Mini 1275

GT also brought the Mini—but not the Cooper models—a further pair of titles in 1978 and 1979 for Longman, for he used some technology from that series (which team-mate Alan Curnow had won), as well as from the Mini-Cooper and S-type days. Of course these titles were obtained in the more restrictive Group '1½' era of British Saloon Car Championship racing, so the 1275 initially went back to the old split Weber layout used by Abingdon for the rally cars (which caused a fuss on the 1968 Monte), rather than to the 8-port cylinder head and fuel injection of the sixties.

The 1275 GT carried on much of Mini-Cooper S racing technology in the British Championship, winning the title for BL in 1978 and 1979

As a postscript it may be interesting to note that those Mini-Cooper S-type racers of the sixties were the most radical works backed cars of all, with the exception of the four wheel drive Minis successfully campaigned in British winter rallycross events of 1971. Even in simple front drive form the Mini was, right up to the late seventies, a front runner in rallycross, a sport that places premium on racing for position instantly and rallying car control qualities. Such success again could be traced back to the Mini Cooper S models—usually developed from 1.3-litres upward and raced with lightweight shells and space frame replacement of front and rear chassis under their skimpy fibreglass, alloy and steel bodies.

Of course Cooper S experience, especially from the 1275 S, is still applied to competition Metros. When I wrote this in 1981, Richard Longman and Alan Curnow were still stoutly dashing through rounds of the British Championship, but their converted non-Hydrolastic suspension of S-type ancestry was mated to Michelin radials rather than Dunlops—and an extra carburettor for Alfa Romeo's Alfasud had made winning as hard as it ever has been in the 22 hectic years that Minis have hurtled round circuits of Britain and Europe.

Overseas the S-type had an equally honourable, but rather misunderstood record. That is not the fault of motoring historians, but of the inherent complications and changes within the premier series, the European Touring Car Championship (ETC). The factory's advertising was a little bit naughty in giving the impression that John Handley was European Touring Car Champion in 1968. He did get more points than anyone else by his winning 1-litre class efforts with a British Vita of Rochdale-970 S, but that year there were no official manufacturers' awards, and so all the

By 1981 the Metro attracted most BL support, but these 1275-engined 'dry' suspension racers (see with Richard Longman chasing Neil McGrath at Silverstone) were beaten for the title by an Alfa Romeo. In Metro trim the four cylinder A-series provided enough power for the aerodynamic shape, but the handling did not have the traditional advantage that Minis showed over their contemporaries in the sixties. The opposition had not been idle!

company could really do was to advertise John Handley as 1-litre Champion and John Rhodes as top dog in the 1600 division.

Overlooked is the fact that Warwick Banks won that European title in 1964. The team that sponsored him was that of Formula 1 owner/manager Ken Tyrrell. He had also used BMC 1-litre engines to propel young Jackie Stewart in Formula 3, hence the connection. Since those days the European Touring Car Championship has been largely uncontested by British-based manufacturers, but the Cooper S has won titles from Canada to America, South Africa, France, Italy, Belgium, Holland right through to Australia and New Zealand.

In fact one BL executive told me that Leyland Australia actually had to back off production of the genuine Cooper S (which continued in KD form after the model's British demise) because Ford and GMH still found it uncomfortably competitive. It's a nice legend for the car that routinely performed the racing giant-killer act, but in truth the Mini Cooper S's racing reputation is tested every weekend somewhere in the World of the 'eighties, and it's a record that still commands my respect without any embellishment.

Mini-Cooper & Cooper S international factory or factory-backed, racing success

Year	Type	Driver	Preparation/entrant	Title
1962	997 Cooper	Love	Cooper Car Co.	1000 cc & overall BRSCC British Champion
1963	1071 S	Whitmore	Cooper Car Co.	BRSCC runner-up
1964	970 S	Banks	Tyrrell Racing Organisation	1000 cc & European Touring Car Champions
1964	1275 S	Fitzpatrick	Cooper Car Co.	1300 cc & BRSCC runner-up
1965	1275 S	Rhodes	Cooper Car Co.	1300 cc & 3rd BRSCC
1965	970 S	Banks	Cooper Car Co.	1000 cc & 2nd BRSCC
1966	1275 S	Rhodes	Cooper Car Co.	1300 cc & runner-up BRSCC
1967	1275 S	Rhodes	Cooper Car Co.	1300 cc & Lombank Entrants' Award
1968	970 S	Handley	British Vita	1000 cc Division 1 European Touring Car Championship
1968	1275 S	Rhodes	Cooper Car Co.	1300 cc Division 2, ETC
1968	1275 S	Rhodes	Cooper Car Co.	1300 cc, RAC Championship
1968	970 S	Spice	Equipe Arden	1000 cc, RAC Championship
1969	970 S	Poole	Equipe Arden	1000 cc & outright RAC Champion

Chapter 6
Rallying:
S for supremacy!

Discuss the Mini and rallying and certain images are bound to form in the mind. Those bouncy little red and white works Coopers whirring through the scenery at enormous speed. Probably heading for another Monte victory and not only waving the flag for Britain, but also making every other rival look rather gross.

With the Abingdon Minis came prominence for the rallying Finns. The effectiveness of Scandinavians in general came as no surprise after the performances of Erik Carlsson and the earlier swift Swedes of the fifties, but the Finns were a revolution on their own. Combined with the Mini and the left foot braking technique that Hannu Mikkola later had to adopt for the Audi Quattro (after years of conventional Ford motoring!), the results were staggering. That is staggering to watch, and staggeringly effective in poor weather, or over loose surfaces—and staggering for cars of 997, 1071, 970 or 1275 cc. Never has so much outright success been garnered by so few litres!

There is only prominent, published authority on the subject—Peter Browning. Having known him since the sixties—he was competition manager at Abingdon from early 1967 to the Stokes closure in 1970, and then worked for his predecessor Stuart

737ABL was an honourable Mini registration. Here Pat Moss (directly behind the bonnet trophy) celebrates victory amongst the ladies on the 1962 Monte Carlo Rally. Her co-driver was Ann Wisdom

Turner—I can say that the Minis were always well administered. However, I know both gentlemen will agree that their success was very largely built on the fine team behind these tiny cars.

Some of the legendary characters within that Abingdon Department—like former deputy foreman Den Green and deputy competition manager Bill Price—only finally moved because of the department's transfer to Cowley in the summer of 1981.

Because of the thoroughness of the Browning book, I do not propose to record the cars' rallying achievements in depth: their record deserves detailed study in its own right, and that is exactly what Browning provided, right down to mechanical specifications, detailed check lists ... truly the works story.

The victory years: 1962–69

When the 997 Cooper arrived, it boosted Abingdon's rallying fortunes immediately to the chance of outright international wins, something that was not possible with the drum-braked 850.

That first international victory came in the 997's second outing, the May 1962 Tulip. Pat Moss and Ann Wisdom were the crew of 737 ABL, a registration plate that did a lot of successful 997 motoring. These ladies had also given the model its competition debut on the January 1962 Monte, where they finished 26th overall and 7th in class.

The 997 was persuaded to provide 70 bhp pretty reliably with help from $\frac{1}{4}$ in. larger SUs ($1\frac{1}{2}$ in. choke), but success was largely derived from the careful assembly of standard parts. So far as the engine went, 7000 rpm was set as a limit, but the standard camshaft, valve sizes and normal 9:1 cr

Private entry on the 1962 Monte displays the high power headlamp and triple auxiliary lamp arrangements then in favour by the factory, as well as screen-mounted 'spotter' lamp

certainly make one nostalgic for yesteryear in today's atmosphere of assorted four wheel drive, mid-engine, turbocharged, rear-gearbox specials needed to win in the eighties. Rallying was meant to prove the quality of the standard product, and in the day of the Mini it did, for if they improved something for competition there was an even chance that the customer would get it free next year—a process that can be clearly traced through the development of 1275 S engine.

The 997 was rallied in works form from January to November 1962, when a trio of them driven on the RAC Rally by the hungry Finnish rivals Timo Makinen and Rauno Aaltonen, were fifth and seventh, with Logan Morrison 13th. By this time

Pat Moss had taken three international wins in a row, so it was no surprise that her astonishing 1-litre should finish third overall on the 1963 Monte, or that all the four 997s entered, finished, including Hopkirk, in sixth place.

Highlights from the Cooper & Cooper S works rallying career

*Between them the 1071 S & 1275 S won the Monte Carlo Rally three times officially and were disqualified (1966) from a fourth win, in the years 1964–67. In 1968 Hopkirk was third.

*The 1274 S won 23 international rallies for the works between its April 1964 Tulip-winning debut and September 1969's assault on the Tour de France. It was succeeded, somewhat patchily, by the 1275 GT Clubman, which used much the same mechanical know-how to finish second on the June 1970 Scottish, Hopkirk's last Abingdon outing.

*Among 1275 S type's results it won: Monte Carlo

Works interior of the mid-sixties shows how they mounted the servo inside. Despite RHD, the car carries a 200 Km/h speedometer while the tachometer is redlined at 8000 rpm. Missing are the Halda navigational aids. Note clear 'second screen' mounted within for maximum demist effect and anti-sizzle gear lever gaiter

Factory Mini-Cooper S
569FMO displays oversize
double SU carburettors and
reshuffled engine bay

Right *The legend in action.
Abingdon prepares Mini-
Cooper S types for the fray in
the 1966/67 period with
service support saloons in the
background, as well as a
veritable horde of the little
red and white Mini terrors*

Above *A helmet-less Hopkirk swings the 1275 S along the Alpine Rally route of 1964. The same car, but driven by Makinen, won the 1965 Monte*

Right *Timo Makinen wheels the S-type to that 1965 Monte win. Wheelarches were modest but so popular that they inspired an appearance on later production non-S-types and were also permitted for use in production classes for racing. A large bore centre exhaust was another widely imitated speed industry item*

(twice), 1000 Lakes (three times); Tulip (twice); Circuit of Ireland (three times); RAC Rally (once); Austrian/Alpine (twice); Acropolis (once); Polish (twice); Geneva (twice); Munich-Vienna-Budapest (twice) and Czechoslovakia (twice).

*The 1071 S won: June 1963 Alpine and January 1964 Monte.

*The 997 Cooper won: Tulip: Baden-Baden and Geneva (all 1962).

*1275 S was second on: RAC; Portugal; Alpine; Marathon de la Route; Rally of the Flowers; Tulip; Circuit of Ireland; Polish; Geneva; Scottish (1275 GT, Gp 6, second 1970 as well).

*997 Cooper was second on: 1963 Tulip.

*1071 S was third on: 1963 Tour de France.

Right *Lighting gets ever
more complicated but
AJB33B was equal to the
demands of carrying the
burly Timo Makinen to third
place on the 1965 Tulip Rally
in 1275 S guise*

*Stuart Turner readeth the
lesson according to the 1966
competitions book to (l to r) a
group including Paul Easter,
Simo Lampinen, Mike Wood,
Rauno Aaltonen, Tony Fall
and Paddy Hopkirk, who had
Makinen turning toward him
and Henry Liddon wearing
glasses behind*

The year of the headlamp fiasco. Timo Makinen/Paul Easter speed to 'victory' in the 1275 works S

Monte Minis from 1964–66 line-up in the Abingdon yard emphasise the yearly changing fashions in lights and heated front screens. On the left is the 1964 car with the 1965 centre AJB44B looking worryingly standard (a show car in this shot? Look at the wheels and large rim steering wheel that could well be standard) while the 1966 specification is shown on the right

*997 Cooper was third on: 1963 Monte Carlo.

*1275 S was third on: Tulip (twice); Monte Carlo; Acropolis; Alpine; Welsh and Swedish.

*Most Mini-Cooper and S-type international works driver wins were scored by:-Rauno Aaltonen (Finland), 9; Paddy Hopkirk (Ireland) & Timo Makinen (Finland) 6 each; Pat Moss & Tony Fall (both UK), 4 each.

Because the 998 Cooper appeared after the introduction of the first S-type (1071 S) it was doomed from the works viewpoint, and I can find no trace of any official works record. However the engine has been used in more restricted and less prestigious events with success and it has proved most amenable to further modification.

Thus the 1071 S took over where the 997 left off?

*Rauno Aaltonen (left) and
Henry Liddon were flown
back with the winning 1275 S
from the 1967 Monte Carlo
Rally. It was the last time the
mighty Mini won the
Monegasque classic*

Not quite, for the 997 lived on usefully some time
after the 1071 S made its international debut in
the hands of Rauno Aaltonen, winning the
Austrian Alpine in June 1963. The last works use
of the 997 I can find was the Austrian Alpine in
June 1964 when Pauline Mayman and Val Domleo
took eighth overall. Aaltonen was fourth in a
1275 S, its third works outing, for Makinen had
christened the car with a win on the Tulip but had
been unsuccessful on the Acropolis.

The effectiveness of the Mini-Coopers—
especially the 1275 S—and the competition 1275
GT—is best assessed from the tabular results. The
cars were certainly well prepared, but towards
the end of their career, it was possible to duplicate
their specification from the BL parts bin. Certainly, it is unlikely that the Monte Carlo Rally
will ever again be won by a car that proved *slower*
than a brand new showroom cousin in back-to-
back tests! Unless the FIA ever decide to go back
to standard car rallying in the interests of
safety/environment, in which case mass-produced
front-drive cars could again dominate the results
list of internationals.

Why did the Coopers start to lose?

At one time in the sixties the Mini-Cooper S
simply looked like the apogee of the all-round
rally car. How could anyone improve on such a
small vehicle with good traction, excellent power
to weight ratio and proven reliability?

The answer was complicated and gradual in
coming, but boiled down to the dawn of cars of
more sporting pedigree (Porsche) or specifically
purpose-built (Alpine-Renault A110, Ford Escort
TC, Lancia Fulvia HF), and a general weakening
of morale, and final withdrawal from an effective
rallying programme by the forces at work on the
unwieldy British Leyland conglomerate.

The Mini-Cooper S did have some more scope

A couple of dry Montes and the advent of ever more powerful opposition from Porsche saw the Minis demoted down the 1968 Monte Carlo Rally order. Here we show Paddy Hopkirk in the fifth-placed 1275 S in Mk II body. Note the plug-in socket for quadruple auxiliary lamps, which allowed faster disentanglement for the vital high speed access to the grille, which was also of a quick-release type

for speed left in it. Later developments of engine size in club formulae proved the point. More work with 12 in. wheels and in general development *could* have postponed the evil day. Yet the fact remains that the 1275 Cooper S scored its last international outright victory on the 1967 Alpine (Paddy Hopkirk/Ron Crellin). It remained a front runner for some time after that, but a dry 1968 Monte that allowed the Porsches to display their 200 bhp speed, plus rear engine traction, must have been a discouragement after years of solid success in the World's most prestigious rally. The works Cooper S-types were third, fourth and fifth in a virtuoso display against the odds. But winning is the works game. . . .

Yet, outside the glamorous works team that is so fondly remembered—save by rivals who should have been winning a couple of years earlier, if they had organised themselves properly—the Mini did just as an effective rallying job.

As in racing, it provided a lot of people with low cost fun. It trained stars like Roger Clark for Ford and set Tony Fall on a career that saw him managing a Monte-Carlo-winning Opel rally team of the eighties. Most British rally stars of the seventies cut their teeth on Minis of one sort or another, and the safe little box (provided the foolish owner doesn't cut too much out of its structure looking for still less weight) is still providing endless fun in club events of the eighties . . . It wouldn't surprise me to see it doing well again in a future energy conscious environment. Even if the badge reads Metro and the specification is sophisticated, some of the technology will have come from Mini-Coopers.

The 1968 works rally 1275 S in non-rally action: ORX77F was unlucky on the Monte of that year, finishing 55th in Makinen's hands. When Aaltonen drove it on the Rally of the Flowers in the same season it had to be retired

Chapter 7
'My part in their history'

It took a long time to swop over from farming to motoring journalism, but when I had made the change the Mini tuning industry was set on its own economic boom. 'Tuners', was the generic phrase, and that meant anything from insulting Downton with such a label, to flattering of some back street butchers.

Yet, whatever their repute, it certainly meant that I sat in a lot of Coopers and S-types. At first thought I surmised that I must have driven most of the machinery we have discussed, but like most Minis, the majority were modified.

Of the standard road cars a factory MK II 1275 S came my way in 1968; a 1071 S from a secondhand car lot in West Sussex, and a Cooper 998 from the office secretary at *Motoring News*.

The 1275 S was in the traditional red with white roof. It provided an outstanding amount of torque relative to size, a point which I proved by towing a broken Ginetta G15 back to the Essex factory behind the S! The constabulary felt that a steady 70 mph for the combination was worthy of a caution, but shared my admiration of the plucky 1275's pulling power....

The standard 1275 S was about the quickest way then available of getting from A to B. When the

Twin Cam Escorts arrived they were certainly a lot faster, approximately 115 mph and 0–60 mph in 9 sec., as against 99 mph in 11 sec. or so for the small Cooper S, but that wasn't the point. The Mini was so small and so safe that it could thread through traffic at a rate unmatched by anything else. A point proved at glamorous length by the antics of the Julienne Remy stunt equipe in the classic film, *The Italian Job*.

Today I would expect 25–28 mpg from a 1275 S, but think it would be hard to put up with the noise levels and the appalling seating/steering wheel relationship of the standard car. You do get used to it, but a degree of modification would be preferable; new seats, a bracket to drop the column and an engine balancing job to make the most of a 1275 under eighties' conditions.

The 1071 S was a very brief outing around the Sussex lanes, but I can remember the green and

Hammersmith coachbuilders Harold Radford were early into the exclusive Mini modifying game. Here you can see that many details have been altered on this Austin Cooper including the door windows, grille, whitewall tyres and full length sunroof set into trimmed roof panel. The interior of some of these modified cars were simply works of art in leather and wood

A 1966 Taurus tuned Mini presented for road test with a typical selection of period accessories. Wooden steering wheel and gear lever knob; 8000 rpm Smiths electronic tachometer and a wooden fascia: this is a non-Cooper, as can be detected from the extension to the standard original 850-style bent lever

white machine was very healthy. It provided an admirable blend of the 970's free-revving nature and yet adequate torque, something the smaller engine lacked. I was impressed enough to want to buy.

Scooting round London looking for non-existent freelance contributions to *Motoring News* was the regular lot of the late production 998 I used to borrow. I seem to remember it had a cloth sunroof and was one of the most enjoyable means of city travel that I can recall. The Hydrolastic suspension was not very clever, allowing a lot of fore and aft pitch. This was

The same Taurus car shows off a brake servo installation

exaggerated by the usual Mini curses—a sticky throttle action, sudden clutch, and the rather fierce way in which the engine would rock within the engine bay, despite the presence of torque reaction bars.

The 998 was always reckoned to be slightly quicker than a 997 and lot more durable. All I remember was that it was nippy enough for the time, but today its performance, and even that of a standard S, would be unlikely to bother something quite unsporting from Fiat or a 1.3-litre Datsun.

In all standard Cooper and Cooper S road tests

that I have read the gearchange is criticised as somewhat sticky, but I remember that the remote control lever did provide a superb change as more miles were accrued.

Modified: from 997 to 1390 cc

By December 1967 modified Minis were beginning to pass through my hands. The first pair were a £600, single Weber 45DCOE Mini-Cooper 997 and a Janspeed-engined Mini Moke 1275 S!

The Moke was hilarious of course, and was used to wriggle round a muddy Sussex field in company with the then FIRST Formula 3 driver Derek Bell. Even with chunkies on the 10 in. wheels, forward progress was slow, so that overheating was the worst problem. Still we did enough together to get a mention in *MN* for *Cars & Car Conversions*, though my time was nine seconds slower than that of Mr Bell, with two Le Mans wins and sundry other international achievements firmly in his future.

Very neat hatchback installation for former Minister of Transport Ernest Marples' Mini-Cooper S, a third door provision made by many of the London specialists

The 997 was a bit rough in the high rpm range, as the long stroke would suggest, but since it also had the racing camshaft 648 or 649, (depending on the period you are talking about—it's the same profile) and larger valves in the head, in a comprehensive conversion job, this was little surprise. Trying to get it to move below 5500 rpm was tricky for this novice (it was my first road test), but the Smiths counter said we had managed 7500 in top on the Firestone-shod 5 in. wide wheels, so there was not too much wrong with it. I chiefly remember the owner turning to talk to me from the wheel as we breasted a rise near Brands Hatch (not Death Hill, but discomfortingly close) at the aforesaid 7500 rpm in fourth. Naturally we

Standard Mini-Cooper in the middle shows one of the most popular Mini conversions of all, the lowline MiniSprint which enjoyed a great deal of sixties support from those devoted to the eternal task of making even the Cooper Minis that little bit different. Anything that reduced the frontal area of the angular Mini shape was welcome from a performance viewpoint, but some of those who imitated the style carried it to the point where the hapless drivers must have felt that they had climbed inside a tank!

Will Sparrow decided that 1.4 litres was the right way to go for this engine in his personal road car of 1971. The engine is in that road and oil-stained condition following a hard session at the track used to originally introduce the Mini in 1959

were in the centre lane and other Sunday traffic was a little perturbed at our sudden appearance.

Lots and lots of 850 Minis filled the intervening months. One was supercharged, and I remember that was in serious trouble before we left the car park! Another had the carburettor sticking through into the engine compartment. I gave up driving it after the flames from an unsuccessful cold start reached into the cabin.

A proper 970 S of 1964, once raced by Jim Edwards (a Renault 5 Champion and leading Fiesta runner by the eighties), arrived at Brands

Hatch as my first track test. That was printed in 1968 (May) *Triple C* and I see that the engine bay was dwarfed by a most enormous Weber 48IDA downdraught of the type that would not look out of place on a Ford GT40 racer of the period.

Complete with a limited slip differential, straight cut gears and a 13:1 compression ratio inside 999 cc this was probably the Mini that convinced me I should never try and compete in one! To this day I have this gap in my competition saloon knowledge, merely reinforced by a 1980 encounter with a 90 bhp 1275 GT that went onto win the 1275

Sparrow's modified 1970 Mk III 1275 S undergoing the stress of road test for Motor Sport in the summer of 1971. The Mini badge has simply taken over from the S-type logo, but this car was beautifully presented, right down to its matching wheelarch extensions and provided some epic cross-country motoring, notable for the mid-range pulling power of the enlarged (1.4 litre) 1275 S engine

The 1967 works Mini-Cooper in single Weber carburated trim. Note the neat dot system for numbering plugs and compact alternator. A model of first class presentation, even by Abingdon standards

Challenge. A competition Mini can be a very twitchy beast: throttling back merely aggravates the original complaint, so you must either have courage and keep the throttle down, or deliberately set it up to oversteer at the flick of a wrist, a condition that the skilled can instantly eliminate by the application of power.

Of the modified 1275s that I tried my favourite was ORX7F, a famous Abingdon registration plate that was then attached to a Special Tuning duplicate of Group 2 rally tune for 1275 S.

Power output was reckoned to be 100 bhp at the flywheel with 84 bhp at the wheels, which indicates the power losses imposed by that gear train. Although ST talked lovingly of duplicating Group 2, there were obvious items on which the works team had first call. Thus a 12:1 cylinder head was listed as limited supply and the use of two $1\frac{1}{2}$ SU carburettors seems suspect as they had been through the split Weber controversy on the Monte by the time (December 1968) my assessment was printed.

Complete with Dunlop 500 L Green Spot racers, which I declined to take off for the road as they were so much fun, wet or dry, we obtained the following acceleration figures (standard figures from the same driver, same track, in brackets): 0–50 mph, 6.2 sec. (8.2 sec.); 0–60 mph, 9.1 sec. (11.6 sec.); 0–70 mph, 13.0 sec. (16.2 sec.); 0–80 mph, 17.4 sec. (24.5 sec.); 0–90 mph, 22.6 sec. (N.A.). Our recorded top speed was 107.1 mph best on the standard 3.765:1 final drive at 7000 rpm compared to just about 100 mph best for a standard 1275 S. Total costs for *all* the Group 2 parts, right down to BMC Rosettes, was £454 9s 9d, and the S then cost £921.

Another memorable S provided by ST at Abingdon had the 1293 cc engine. Complete with four Amal monobloc motorcycle carburettors it was

Now, that is what we can called tuned! A number of subsidiary changes were needed before Abingdon could cram the front of Makinen's 1967-intended RAC Rally Mini with the Lucas injection equipment normally used for racing. The event was cancelled, leaving Ford also with some spare fuel injected machinery

The 1974 Mini 1275 GT showing how the 12 in diameter wheels did eventually reach the man in the street. Unfortunately the GT was never more than a pale echo of the Cooper S

claimed to give 124 bhp—about the same as they were getting from the works aluminium 8-port cylinder head with Webers on the four wheel-drive rallycross cars.

As with any other Mini equipped with straight cut gears, the chief impressions were of sheer speed with which you could 'swop cogs' as we then put it ... and the noise! Add four open slide Amals, and the row within was matched only by the sheer exhilaration of trying to keep on the road with a power unit that was either 'on' or 'off'.

By contrast a Wood & Pickett Mini 1275 was tried for a few surburban miles in the late seventies, and I could see why so many pop stars and the like had opted for these small luxury

Is it all going to happen
again with Metro? Yes, it
seems quite likely, but the
badge would not be Cooper
but MG as things stood in
early 1982. Whispers suggest
something even faster too. Its
cover had not been blown at
publication

Inside the Metro Cooper of
1981 and we can see that the
Cooper driver expects a lot
more civilisation around
him/her. Fresh air vents and
clear instrumentation in
front of the driver, whatever
will they think of next?

carriages. A whisper of wind round the hair from the full length folding roof, a mutter from the sound-deadened engine bay (aided by lush carpeting and a young forest's worth of wood inside) and the Cooper S became almost civilised. Luckily it still bobbed up and down on its suspension with impish delight, scuttled through corners in the traditional manner and muttered through its transfer and production gearbox.

Drive a Mini today—particularly a Cooper or S-type—and the smile that spreads across your features just cannot be prevented. To live with it, as we did then, would be hell after two decades as progress. Nevertheless, for fun at a very reasonable price, you still can't beat a Cooper.

The S-types offer the same excellence of £-per-silly-grin ratio, but those who want to keep the vehicles in original condition will find this is a harder task than for the Cooper 998. Cooper or Cooper S, this stubby sporting pioneer should occupy the smallest space and highest affection of any postwar collection to its owner.

Specifications

Specifications of all Mini-Cooper and S-type production cars

**Austin & Morris
Cooper 997 (1961–64)**

Engine: BMC A-series four cylinder derivative, ohv, transversely mounted, water cooled, Type 9F.
Capacity: bore × stroke, 62.43 mm × 81.28 mm = 997 cc.
Compression: 9:1 (optional 8.3:1)
Valve sizes: inlet, 29.4 mm; exhaust, 25.4 mm. Lift, 7.92 mm.
Carburation: twin SU HS2, 31.75 mm choke diameter. Wire air cleaners (2).
Performance: 55 bhp at 6000 rpm; 54 lb ft. at 3600 rpm; 134 psi. BMEP at 3500 rpm.
Transmission: single dry plate $7\frac{1}{8}$ in. clutch, helical gear final drive from transverse gearbox.
Ratios: 3.765 final drive (std), 3.44:1 (common option others available). Standard gear ratios: 1st, 12.05:1; 2nd, 7.213:1; 3rd, 5.11:1; 4th, direct. Option: 1st, 11.03:1; 2nd, 6.598:1; 3rd, 4.674:1; 4th, direct.
Brakes: disc, 7 in. diameter (front) with two types of boost assistance in production. Rear—7 in. diameter by $1\frac{1}{4}$ in. wide drum.
Wheels & tyres: 10 in. diameter × 3.5 in. rim, pressed steel with (1961) Dunlop Gold Seal Dunlop nylon 5.20 crossplies.
Suspension: IFS via transverse wishbones and Moulton rubber springs. Irs through trailing arms and Moulton rubber springs. Telescopic dampers front and rear.
Standard equipment: 100 mph central speedometer, non-decimal total mileage, with two smaller Smiths electrical gauges for oil pressure (pressure relief, 70 psi.) and water temperature. Pile carpet with underfelt, leathercloth seats and two spoke plastic wheel.
Body: Six duotone colour choices (roof panel is contrast colour) weighing 635 kg/1400 lbs approx.
Length: 10 ft. $\frac{1}{4}$ in. (3.05 metres)
Wheelbase: 6 ft. $\frac{5}{32}$ in. (2.037 m)
Height: 4 ft. 5 in. (1.35 m)
Width: 4 ft. $7\frac{1}{2}$ in. (1.41 m)

Track: 3 ft. 11$\frac{17}{32}$ in. (1.205 m) F
3 ft. 9$\frac{7}{8}$ in. (1.164 m) R
Options: limited competition equipment, radio and fresh air heater.

Austin & Morris Cooper 998 (1964–69)

Engine: Principles as 997, Type 9 FA.
Capacity: bore × stroke, 64.588 mm × 76.20 mm = 998 cc.
Compression: 9:1 (optional 7.8:1)
Valve sizes: inlet, 30.86 mm; exhaust and lift, as 997.
Carburation: as 997 but standard GY needles replaced GZ.
Performance: 55 bhp at 5800 rpm; 57 lb ft. at 3000 rpm; 142 psi. BMEP at 3000 rpm.
Transmission: As 997 but with synchromesh 1st gear in 1968. Optional 3.44:1 final drive (as before) allows 16.05 mph per 1000 rpm instead of 14.7 mph of 3.765:1. Diaphragm spring clutch, late 1964.
Ratios: as above.
Brakes: No booster, smaller bore master cylinder and larger reservoir.
Wheels & tyres: SP41 radials became standard two months after 998 launch.
Suspension: Hydrolastic damping introduced after 6 months 998 production.
Standard equipment: Driveshaft couplings, radiator, oil seal and gearbox improved in production life.
Body: as 997 until late 1967 when Mk II body with larger rear window, revised grille, trim and larger rear lamps (squared off).
Options: Possible Special Tuning Department (Abingdon) competition-orientated modifications, many in common with other Minis. Reclining seat option from late 1965 and heated rear window Spring 1969.

Austin & Morris Mini-Cooper 1071 S (1963-64)

Engine: Further strengthened A-series derivative with nitrided crankshaft & offset bores. Type, 10F, engine number prefixed 9FSAH
Capacity: bore × stroke, 70.60 mm × 68.26 mm = 1071 cc.
Compression: 9:1
Valve sizes: inlet, 35.71 mm; exhaust, 30.96 mm. Lift, as 997.
Carburation: As 997/998 but with H6 needles
Performance: 70 bhp at 6000 rpm; 62 lb ft. torque at 4500 rpm; 146 psi BMEP at 3500–5000 rpm.

Transmission: As 997/998, with same final drive (3.765:1) and optional 3.444:1. More options & special equipment including straight cut gears available from factory. Bonded clutch linings (riveted) with double pressure springs (12 instead of 6).
Brakes: $7\frac{1}{2}$ in. diameter disc (F) and 997/998 drum rear with Lockheed Hydrovac servo assistance.
Wheels & tyres: usually ventilated round hole steel wheels, 4.5 in. rim × 10 in. with 145-10 SP41 Dunlops: some 5.50 × 10 in. Dunlop SP.
Suspension: All Moulton rubber principle in production run.
Standard equipment: Fresh air heater (standardised on Cooper too at intro of S) and 120 mph speedo, otherwise as Cooper, though oil pressure relief set at 75 psi.
Body: Frequently duotone red/white or green/white roof. Weight, 640 kg/1411 lbs.
Dimensions: as Cooper except for:-
Track, front 4 ft. $\frac{17}{32}$ in. (1.233 m).
Track, rear: 3 ft. $\frac{5}{16}$ in. (1.202 m). Both with $4\frac{1}{2}$ in. rim fitted, $3\frac{1}{2}$ in. standard wheel also optional when dimensions as Cooper/Mini saloons.
Options: second $5\frac{1}{2}$ gallon fuel tank, 3.44:1 final drive, close ratio gearbox. Wide range of factory competition parts.

Austin & Morris Mini-Cooper 970 S (1964–65)

Engine: short stroke variant of S-type A-series. Engine prefix, 9FSAX Domed pistons.
Capacity: bore × stroke, 70.64 mm × 61.91 mm = 970 cc. Type, 9F.
Compression ratio: 9.75:1
Valve sizes: as 1071 S
Carburation: as 1071 S, needle change.
Performance: 65 bhp at 6500 rpm 55 lb ft. torque at 3500 rpm.
Transmission: as 1071 S but diaphragm clutch from mainstream production.
Brakes: As 1071 S
Wheels & tyres: as 1071 S
Suspension: same principles as 1071 S but Hydrolastic damping instead of rubber & telescopic dampers.
Standard equipment: As 1071 S
Body: As 1071 S
Options: As 1071 S, fresh air heater standard.

Austin & Morris Mini-Cooper S, also Mk III Mini-badged 1275 S (1964–71)

Engine: long stroke S-type, A-series derivative. Prefix, 9 FSAY

Capacity: bore × stroke, 70.64 mm × 81.33 mm = 1275 cc. Type, 12F.

Compression ratio: 9.5:1

Valve sizes: As 1071/970 S & lift.

Carburation: As 1071/970 S, needle change.

Performance: 76 bhp at 5800 rpm; 79 lb ft. torque at 3000 rpm.

Transmission: Initially as 1071/970, but protracted 1967–68 introduction of all synchromesh gearbox. Diaphragm spring clutch, as 970 S, introduced after five months production.

Brakes: As 1071/970 S.

Wheels & tyres: As with 970 S introduced with 145-10 Dunlop SP41 radials.

Suspension: Originally Moulton rubber, changed for hydrolastic damping after five months production. Uprated Hydrolastic, Spring 1966 & for remainder of run. All independent wishbone front and trailing arm rear.

Standard equipment: A 130 mph speedometer otherwise originally as 970 S Late 1964 introduction of three-position drilled seat brackets. Early 1966 intro of oil cooler and optional second tank made standard. Autumn 1967 change to Mk II body shared with 998 Cooper. Spring 1970 into final Mk III body with wind-up windows etc (see below).

Body: increasing use of non-duotone paint and available in standard colours of model year. Body changes referred to above detail as: Mk II, wider rear window, larger front grille with bolder chrome frame, revised badging, improved seats and squared-off taillights. Mk III, ADO 20 bodystyle, with winding windows, concealed door hinges and Clubman trim for doors (no more big bins for storage!) further seating revision.

Dimensions: As other Cooper S, save 11 gallon fuel capacity standard in place of 5½ gallon from early 1966.

Options: Reclining seats from late 1964; 3.44:1 final drive; limited slip differential; heated rear window (from Spring 1969). Very wide range of replacement competition-orientated parts from Abingdon to the point where Group 2 works rally car could almost be duplicated (1968).

Production changes 1961–1971

October 1961:	Original 997 Austin or Morris Cooper introduced with Mini Super body trim, long stroke, twin carb engine and 7 in. diameter front disc brakes. 55 bhp/85 mph.
March 1963	From Chassis no L/A257 313830 (RHD) and C/A 257L 212740 (LHD), small bore master cylinder and bigger reservoir with normal Mini front brake line to replace pressure booster in the hydraulic piping to front discs of original Coopers.
March 1963:	Original Austin and Morris Mini-Cooper S announced. Body & trim like Cooper, but far stronger engine, larger front disc brakes (with servo-assistance), wider wheels. 70 bhp/92 mph.
February 1964:	Wiper arcs modified on all Minis to avoid screen rubber.
January 1964:	Mini-Cooper 997 replaced by shorter stroke 998 engine. Same bhp, slightly more torque & performance.
March 1964:	Austin or Morris versions 970 and 1275 cc Mini-Cooper S-types obtained by short and long stroke derivatives of original 1071 S with same running gear. 970. 65 bhp/90 mph and 1275, 75 bhp/99 mph.
	SP41 radial standard on Cooper and some Cooper S, though 1071 S originally had radial SP of chunkier tread.
July 1964	All Coopers get lower pressure setting for rear brake anti-lock valve.
August 1964:	1071 S stopped production.
September 1964:	Hydrolastic suspension and trim changes.
	New gear change forks with larger contact area from engine number, 9 FD SA H 1071.
	Diaphragm spring clutch for 998 from: 9 F SA H 3780
	Diaphragm spring clutch for 970 from: 9F SA X 29001
	Diaphragm spring clutch for 1071 from: 9F SA H 33260
	Diaphragm spring clutch for 1275 from: 9F SA Y 31001
	Positive crankcase venting, 970 S, from: 9FD X 29004
	Positive crankcase venting 998 Cooper from: 9FD SA H 33261
	Positive crankcases venting, 1275 S from: 9FD SA Y 31406
October 1964:	Bigger rubber for driveshaft couplings, Cooper 998.
November 1964:	All Coopers get three position seat brackets, driver only.
January 1965:	970 S stopped production.
	998 gets more efficient radiator (13 gills per in. instead of 16 gills).
May 1965:	Better scroll-type oil seal for primary gears from: 9FD SA H 6448

Nov/Dec 1965:	Gradual introduction of reclining seat option for all Coopers.
January 1966:	1275 S gets twin tanks, oil cooler, standard. Safety bosses fitted under leading edge of exterior door handle.
April/May 1966:	1275 S gets higher rate Hydrolastic with steel/rubber bushing for lower wishbones. Taper roller bearings in rear hubs. Solid universal for inboard end of driveshaft. Stronger suspension mountings. From: Austin car no, C/A 257 851199 and Morris, K/A 254 851028
October 1967:	All Coopers (1275 S & Cooper 998) go into Mk II shell with larger rear windows, Mini Super de luxe trim, squared rear lamps etc. Gradual 100 per cent fit of synchromesh 1st gear box completed during next 12 months, all Coopers and S-type.
April/May 1969:	Adoption of heated rear window option.
November 1969:	Mini-Cooper 998 stopped production.
October 1969:	Mini 1275 GT introduced. Single carburettor 1275 engine (not identical to S within either), front disc brakes, extra instrumentation (rev counter!), Rostyle wheels, Hydrolastic suspension, S-type front discs. Gets 12 in. wheels, 1974. 60 bhp/86 mph.
March 1970:	1275 S goes into Mk III (ADO20) concealed hinge, wind-up window Mini shell with Clubman trim of seats & doors & Hydrolastic.
Oct/Nov 1970:	Ignition shield fitted from car no, N20 D 538A
July 1971:	Mk III Mini-Cooper 1275 S ceased production in UK. Some KD in Australia.

Production

After I had written the book a new set of figures from 'a dark corner at Longbridge,' came to light through a leading authority on Mini matters.

These figures, based on the October-October financial year of the company do not quite tie into other accounts of Mini production but are interesting enough—and more detailed than any that I have seen published before—so I reproduce them first.

Mini-Cooper 997 & 998, Austin and Morris variants.

	Home	Export	Year total	Overall total
1960–61	10	-	10	10
1961–62	5433	4554	9987	9997
1962–63	6062	5448	11,510	21,507
1963–64	4093	5088	9181	30,688
1964–65	3637	5121	8758	39,446
1965–66	4907	6748*	11,655	51,101

*Unfortunately 1966–69 (998) completion of record could not be unearthed. By subtracting the grand total of 51,101 given here from the total figure of 101,242 Mini-Coopers (1961–69) given at the time Mini broke 3 million overall production, it is merely possible to say that the figure of 101,242 total Cooper production is awfully high for 1967, 1968 and 1969, averaging 16,713 units pa. *More* than given for a single previous year, and contributing a further 50,141 units over that three years. Mini-Cooper 997 production was approximately 25,000 units.

From the same source, an analysis of 1962–1966 Mini-Cooper S-type production. Only the 1275 S went beyond this period, so we can state with some authority that S-type total production broke down as follows.

```
 970 S (1964–65)    976 units
1071 S (1962–64) 4017 units
1275 S (1964–71) 40,449 units.
```

The 1962–1966 analysis, S-type only, in detail :-

	Home	Export /KD	Total	Overall Total
1962–63	442	74	516	516
1963–64	2509	1833	4342	4858
1964–65	2978	2374	5352	10,210
1965–66	1142	3086	4228	14,438

By marque, Austin or Morris, analysis shows a pretty even split with 2133 1071 S Austins produced, compared with 1884 Morris 1071 S, or 489 Austin 970 S and 487 Morris 970 S. Because of the dating, no final analysis could be given of 1275 S.

Again, one is forced to wonder at the total Cooper S production figure given on 25 October, 1972, which reported 44, 859 total production for all S-types. For 1962–66 had produced only 14,438 S-types. Thus 1967–71 (plus some strays from Australia that carried on after production ceased in UK, but not on any great scale) should have seen some 30,421 S-types made, or an average 6084 pa, again more than the highest yearly output shown for 1962–1966.

In those days one had to take into account Innocenti and some overseas assembly (particularly of Cooper 998 and 1275 S) and it may be that, when all these totals had struggled in over subsequent years the grand totals became reality.

Once more, official totals for the types given in October 1972 were:
Mini Cooper 998 & 977: 44,859
Mini-Cooper S, 970, 1071 & 1275: 101,242.

Acknowledgements

Apart from author Jeremy Walton's personal acknowledgements all of which are mentioned through the text, illustrative acknowledgements are fairly short since the largest source of photographs is quite simply British Leyland. Various of their archives were raided and all were co-operative. Thank you.

Others helped to complete the picture. The National Motor Museum provided a major selection of those not coming from BL while the important remainder came from *Autosport*, Mirco Decet, Dunlop Limited, Ray Holman, LAT, Dr C. B. Mynott, Fred Scatley and G. Willmott.

The Mini-Cooper Club, an owners' club for all Mini enthusiasts, helped photographer Mirco Decet with cars and locations. Their address is 9 Walesbeach, Furnace Green, Crawley, West Sussex RH10 6SJ.

Index